The —
LITTLE BOOK OF
STOICISM

Rasha Barrage

summersdale

THE LITTLE BOOK OF STOICISM

An Hachette UK Company
www.hachette.co.uk

Summersdale Publishers
Part of Octopus Publishing Group Limited
Carmelite House
50 Victoria Embankment
LONDON
EC4Y 0DZ
UK

www.summersdale.com

The authorized representative in the EEA is Hachette Ireland, 8 Castlecourt Centre, Dublin 15, D15 XTP3, Ireland (email: info@hbgi.ie)

Printed and bound in Poland

ISBN: 978-1-83799-627-8
eISBN: 978-1-83799-628-5

This FSC® label means that materials and other controlled sources used for the product have been responsibly sourced

MIX
Paper | Supporting responsible forestry
FSC® C018236

Substantial discounts on bulk quantities of Summersdale books are available to corporations, professional associations and other organizations. For details contact general enquiries: telephone: +44 (0) 1243 771107 or email: enquiries@summersdale.com.

Contents

Introduction

Have you ever pondered life's deeper questions, like the meaning of existence or your true purpose? If so, you'll likely feel a strong connection with Stoicism. This ancient philosophy, originating in Ancient Greece and rooted in practicality and wisdom, offers timeless guidance for navigating life's challenges with grace and resilience.

Far from being an obscure, academic discipline, Stoicism is a vibrant, living philosophy that has inspired people for over 2,000 years. In a world often marked by fear and uncertainty, Stoicism provides a clear, empowering framework for living well.

At its core, Stoicism teaches self-mastery: that you can't control external events, but you can control how you respond to them. The philosophy details the small but profound steps for achieving personal growth, encouraging the cultivation of wisdom, courage, temperance and justice (Stoicism's core virtues).

In this book, you'll journey through the history of Stoicism, exploring its key figures, principles and all-important virtues. By the end, you'll understand how this ancient philosophy can help you achieve tranquillity of mind and *eudaimonia* – a life well lived.

Philosophy's Golden Age

In Ancient Greece, philosophy wasn't just an academic discipline; it was the foundation of intellectual and civic life. Unlike today, where philosophy is often confined to universities, in the Classical Era of Greece (fifth to fourth century BCE), it shaped public life, politics and personal conduct.

It was during this Golden Age that Athens became a hub of philosophical enquiry, with thinkers like Socrates, Plato and Aristotle creating standards for contemplating life's big questions. One of the key figures during the period was Heraclitus, whose idea of the *logos*, or a rational principle guiding the cosmos, later became central to Stoicism.

Following this, the Hellenistic period emerged after the death of Alexander the Great in 323 BCE, spreading Greek culture (and its love of philosophy) across civilizations in Egypt, the Middle East and Europe. This era saw the fusion of Greek and Eastern traditions, creating a rich intellectual environment that nurtured the development of Stoicism and other schools of thought.

A timeline of the key thinkers and founders

THALES OF MILETUS (*c.*624–*c.*546 BCE)
Greek philosopher from Miletus (near Söke in present-day Turkey), often regarded as "the first philosopher".

HERACLITUS (*c.*540–*c.*480 BCE)
Greek philosopher from Ephesus (now Selçuk, present-day Turkey).

SOCRATES (*c.*469–399 BCE)
Greek philosopher from Athens.

PLATO (*c.*427–*c.*347 BCE)
Greek philosopher from Athens. Student of Socrates. Founded the Academy in Athens (c.387 BCE).

DIOGENES OF SINOPE (*c.*412–323 BCE)
Greek philosopher and key figure in Cynicism. Disciple of Antisthenes, a student of Socrates.

ARISTOTLE (384–322 BCE)
Greek philosopher from Stagira. Student of Plato at the Academy. Founded the Lyceum in Athens (335 BCE).

CRATES OF THEBES (*c.*365–*c.*285 BCE)
Greek Cynic philosopher who taught Zeno of Citium.

ZENO OF CITIUM (*c.*334–262 BCE)

Greek philosopher. Founded Stoicism; taught that the goal of life was "to live consistently".

CLEANTHES OF ASSOS (*c.*330–*c.*230 BCE)

Greek Stoic. Succeeded Zeno. Wrote *Hymn to Zeus*.

CHRYSIPPUS OF SOLI (*c.*279–*c.*206 BCE)

Greek Stoic. Student of Cleanthes. Systematized Stoicism.

PANAETIUS OF RHODES (*c.*185–*c.*110 BCE)

Greek Stoic. Helped introduce Stoicism to Rome.

POSIDONIUS OF APAMEA (*c.*135–*c.*51 BCE)

Greek Stoic. Student of Panaetius. Explored ethics, cosmology and psychology.

SENECA (*c.*4 BCE–65 CE)

Roman Stoic. Advisor to Nero.

EPICTETUS (*c.*55–135 CE)

Roman Stoic and former slave. Teachings compiled in *Discourses*.

MARCUS AURELIUS (121–180 CE)

Roman emperor and Stoic philosopher. Wrote *Meditations*.

Heraclitus

Heraclitus, a pre-Socratic philosopher, believed that everything in the universe changes, opposites are interconnected and life is governed by the universal principle of *logos*. This idea of *logos* – a rational, divine order of the universe – became a cornerstone of Stoic philosophy.

Early founders of Stoicism drew from his belief in the cyclical nature of change and the importance of reason in understanding the world. They integrated *logos* into their ethical system, teaching that living in harmony with this natural, rational order leads to a virtuous, fulfilling life (see p.68). For the Stoics, as with Heraclitus, change and challenges were not to be feared but embraced as part of the natural flow of life. To live in harmony with nature means accepting life (and death) as it unfolds, aligning our actions and desires with our human need for connection and recognizing the underlying order amid constant change.

Heraclitus believed opposites, like life/death or awake/sleep, are essential to the universe's balance, with conflict driving change and harmony. The Stoics adapted these ideas, viewing conflict and adversity as natural, essential elements for personal growth.

Socrates

There's been no figure more influential to Stoicism than Socrates. Living in ancient Athens, he urged people to prioritize virtue over wealth, power or fame. For Socrates, virtue was a state of understanding or deep awareness that guides moral behaviour. His famous declaration, "The unexamined life is not worth living", embodies the Stoic quest for self-improvement and wisdom. In Plato's *Republic*, Socrates discusses four virtues – courage, moderation (or temperance), wisdom and justice. These virtues are attributed not only to individuals but also to the ideal city. He suggests that when these virtues are present in the city, it becomes "completely good" or functions harmoniously.

Socrates spoke of philosophy as care of the soul and believed knowledge and virtue go hand in hand. This deeply influenced Stoic thinkers, who saw philosophy as therapy and virtue as the key to fulfilment.

Socrates' calm acceptance of his death sentence in 399 BCE (for charges of impiety and corrupting the youth) exemplified the Stoic ideal of facing life's challenges with courage and composure.

Plato

Plato, a student of Socrates, agreed with the idea that the *eudaimonic* (well-lived) life is achieved by cultivating wisdom and prioritizing the soul's health. Plato viewed wisdom and knowledge as key to living a good life, a concept that Stoics embraced wholeheartedly.

While the Stoics rejected Plato's idea of an immortal, tripartite soul (made up of reason, spirit and desire), they adopted his belief that true happiness comes from inner harmony and unity. In pursuit of this balance, practices like journalling (see p.73) and voluntary discomfort (see p.81) were actively practised and encouraged. The Stoics believed that such activities foster inner coherence and lead to a fulfilled life.

Zeno of Citium, the founder of Stoicism, studied at Plato's Academy for over a decade. It was a place for students (known as "Academics") to explore big questions about life, justice and the cosmos. In many ways, Stoicism is a continuation of Plato's quest for wisdom but with an emphasis on a practical application to everyday challenges.

Aristotle

Aristotle was a philosopher who explored so many topics that, by the Middle Ages, he was considered *the* philosopher. A student of Plato, he made contributions to many areas, including biology, ethics, politics, logic and theatre.

He believed the human ability to reason sets us apart from other animals, and it is by using this reason that we can live virtuous, fulfilled lives.

Aristotle also argued that humans are social creatures by nature, designed to live in communities and contribute to the common good. This idea fed directly into the Stoic belief in justice as a virtue and the conviction that individuals should act for the greater good of humanity, not just their own self-interest.

He believed happiness, or *eudaimonia*, isn't a fleeting feeling but the result of living in accordance with one's full potential over an entire lifetime; something that can only be evaluated once life is complete. The Stoics similarly focused on cultivating virtue and a well-lived life through continuous effort.

The Cynics

Cynicism, one of Ancient Greece's most unconventional schools of thought, gained its name from the Greek word *kynikos*, meaning "dog-like", or *kyôn*, meaning "dog". Though there's debate on how exactly this term came to represent the Cynics, many scholars believe it was initially a slur aimed at their defiant and often bizarre behaviour. Cynic philosophers lived in extreme simplicity, disregarding social norms to the point of openly engaging in acts like public defecation – similar to the behaviour of stray dogs. Yet for the Cynics, this lifestyle wasn't mere eccentricity; it was a radical rejection of societal expectations.

The Cynics believed true happiness was found not in wealth, reputation or possessions but in self-sufficiency, virtue and living simply and freely in nature. Living virtuously meant focusing only on life's essentials. Diogenes of Sinope, perhaps the most famous Cynic, took this philosophy to its extreme. He chose to live in a barrel, mocked social customs and even roamed the streets of Athens with a lantern "searching for an honest man". His disdain for wealth and power, along with his contempt for superficial social values, challenged the norms of Greek society.

By embracing poverty and a disregard for public decorum, the Cynics advocated a life free of material desire and false pretences. Their approach heavily influenced the founders of Stoicism, particularly Zeno of Citium, who reportedly studied with Crates, a prominent Cynic philosopher. The Stoics adopted Cynicism's emphasis on inner freedom and resilience, though they developed it into a more structured and practical ethical system. Where Cynicism promoted extreme asceticism and a rejection of all social conventions, Stoicism took a more moderate stance. Stoics valued similar virtues, such as self-discipline and rationality, but believed that one could engage with society while maintaining inner detachment and virtue.

AN EVOLVING WORD

The term "cynical" as we use it today – suggesting distrust or negativity towards others' motives – evolved around the eighteenth century. Thinkers of that time admired the ancient Cynics' challenge to social norms and their critique of greed. Yet, as "cynical" became more common in language, it narrowed to imply a jaded view of human behaviour. This limited definition doesn't capture the Cynics' broader philosophy, which prioritized happiness through independence and a life free from society's superficial values.

Diogenes of Sinope

Diogenes of Sinope, known as "Diogenes the Cynic", was a philosopher famed for his eccentric lifestyle and sharp criticisms of social conventions. Born in the fifth century BCE in Sinope (in present-day Turkey), Diogenes moved to Athens and became a student of Antisthenes, who had himself been a student of Socrates. Diogenes pushed Antisthenes' teachings to an extreme, embracing a life of poverty, simplicity and utter rejection of social norms. He believed that virtue was best achieved by living in harmony with nature, which meant freeing oneself from societal conventions, such as wealth, status and even modesty.

Diogenes' unusual lifestyle drew much attention, as did his sharp wit and unabashed criticism of society's hypocrisy, materialism and moral corruption. One of the most famous stories of his life involves his encounter with Alexander the Great, who, intrigued by Diogenes' reputation, visited him in Corinth. Standing over the philosopher, Alexander offered to grant any wish Diogenes desired. Unimpressed by the conqueror's fame and power, Diogenes merely replied, "Stand out of my sunlight."

Hellenistic period

The death of Alexander the Great in 323 BCE – and Aristotle's just a year later – marked a transformative moment in Greek history, signalling the beginning of the Hellenistic period, which would last until Roman dominance in 31 BCE. This period brought significant shifts in Greek culture and philosophy as Greek influence and ideas spread throughout the Mediterranean, Egypt and parts of Asia. With the sudden fragmentation of Alexander's empire, traditional philosophical ideas were re-examined and adapted to address the complexities of a vast, interconnected world.

Instead of the abstract, theoretical questions that characterized the Classical period under Socrates, Plato and Aristotle, Hellenistic philosophers focused on practical approaches for coping with life's uncertainties and challenges. Cynicism, popularized by Diogenes of Sinope, epitomized this turn towards personal resilience and independence from social conventions, rejecting wealth and status in favour of a simple, self-sufficient life. This shift towards practicality prepared the way for Stoicism to become the era's most influential philosophy, offering much-needed guidance for navigating a rapidly changing world.

Zeno of Citium

Zeno of Citium's journey to founding Stoicism began, as many great stories do, with a twist of fate. Zeno was a wealthy merchant from Citium, Cyprus, but his life took an unexpected turn when he was shipwrecked near Athens around 314 BCE.

Stranded, and with his fortune lost to the sea, Zeno wandered up to a bookseller's stall and stumbled upon a copy of Xenophon's *Memorabilia*, a text about Socrates' life and teachings. Fascinated, he asked the bookseller where he could meet a real philosopher, and by remarkable coincidence, Crates of Thebes, the leading Cynic philosopher, walked by at that very moment!

Zeno went on to study with Crates and other prominent philosophers of the time, including other Cynics (see p.14) and Academics (see p.12). While he admired their teachings, especially the Cynics' emphasis on living in accordance with nature and denying societal excess, Zeno sought a more structured, balanced approach. After years of learning from others, he eventually broke away and began teaching his own philosophy in the Agora of Athens – specifically in the *stoa poikilê*, or "painted porch". It was here that Stoicism, named after this famous location, was born.

Unlike the Cynics, who were known for avoiding material comforts, Zeno's philosophy didn't demand a rejection of society. Instead, he emphasized personal virtue and emotional resilience, and encouraged individuals to embrace the principles of nature, cultivate reason (mastering emotions through logic) and practise self-control. According to Zeno, *pathos* (an irrational, excessive response to external impressions) "is a disturbance of the mind repugnant to reason, and against Nature". For him, happiness wasn't found in wealth or fame but in living a life aligned with virtue and reason – values that people could control even amid external chaos.

Zeno's teachings resonated deeply with those living in the turbulent Hellenistic world. Stoicism quickly grew in popularity, spreading beyond the painted porch and influencing not just the educated elite but also soldiers, slaves and statesmen alike. It was a philosophy for everyone, offering a path to inner peace and moral clarity, regardless of one's external circumstances.

I made a prosperous voyage when I suffered shipwreck.

Zeno of Citium, in Diogenes Laertius'
Lives of Eminent Philosophers

Three phases of Stoicism

Over time, Stoicism developed through three distinct phases, expanding and adapting to new challenges and audiences:

- **Early Stoa** – This initial phase began with Zeno in the third century BCE and included thinkers such as Cleanthes and Chrysippus, who developed core Stoic doctrines. Chrysippus, in particular, shaped much of Stoic logic and ethics, solidifying Stoicism as a coherent philosophical system.
- **Middle Stoa** – During this period, Stoicism spread beyond Greece. Key figures like Panaetius and Posidonius integrated Stoic philosophy with broader Hellenistic and Roman ideas, making Stoicism more practical for political and social life. Panaetius was known for moderating some of the more rigid aspects of early Stoicism.
- **Late Stoa** – This phase is best known through the teaching of Epictetus and the writings of Roman Stoics such as Seneca and Marcus Aurelius. They emphasized personal ethics and resilience in the face of life's difficulties. Marcus Aurelius, a Roman emperor, left behind *Meditations*, which remains one of the most influential Stoic texts to this day.

MEET
THE STOICS

Stoicism is far more than an abstract philosophy confined to scholars; it's a way of life that's been embraced by some of the most influential figures in history. From emperors to slaves, these individuals lived by Stoic principles, shaping its course and proving its timeless relevance. In this chapter, you'll explore the backgrounds of key Stoic philosophers, how they encountered Stoicism and the unique insights they contributed to this enduring philosophy.

You'll meet Cleanthes, who succeeded Zeno and worked tirelessly to preserve and expand Stoic teachings. You'll also look at Cato the Younger, known for his unshakeable integrity and resistance to tyranny, and Seneca, whose writings on resilience and self-discipline continue to inspire modern readers. Each of these figures, along with several others to whom you'll be introduced, had a unique path to Stoicism, discovering its teachings at different stages of life and in the midst of diverse personal struggles.

Through their stories, you'll see how Stoicism became a timeless guide to navigating life's challenges. By the end of this chapter, you'll have a deeper understanding of how these remarkable individuals used Stoic wisdom to shape both their personal lives and the world around them.

The school of the porch

Zeno of Citium founded the Stoic school in Athens around 300 BCE, quickly earning a reputation as a brilliant teacher. Zeno's followers were first known as "Zenonians", but over time they became known as "Stoics", based on the *stoa poikilê*, where they met and poets once assembled (see p.18). Zeno's teachings attracted followers from all walks of life, drawn to his emphasis on virtue, rationality and resilience.

Diogenes Laertius, a biographer of the Greek philosophers, preserved summaries of Zeno's ideas, revealing his division of philosophy into logic, physics (defined as the study of the natural world) and ethics (see p.53).

The Athenians held Zeno in high esteem, honouring him with keys to the city walls and a golden crown. After his death in *c.*262 BCE, the Stoic school flourished well beyond the confines of the physical *stoa*, spreading its teachings across the ancient world and shaping the course of Western philosophy. Unlike other schools of philosophy named after their founders, the Stoics chose a name reflecting their intellectual ideals rather than a personal legacy.

Cleanthes of Assos

Cleanthes, a pivotal figure in the development of Stoicism, was born around 330 BCE in Assos (in present-day Turkey). Initially a successful boxer, he arrived in Athens with just four drachmae in his pocket, determined to find a deeper understanding of life. By day, he learned under Crates the Cynic and Zeno, and by night, he worked as a water carrier, to support himself. His fellow students, noting his slow but persistent nature, nicknamed him "the Ass". Cleanthes embraced the title as it implied that his back was strong enough to bear the weight of Zeno's teachings.

Cleanthes' dedication to philosophical studies even drew the attention of the courts, who suspected him of having secret financial support. When Cleanthes proved he worked at night to fund his studies, the judges were so impressed that they offered him money – which he refused.

After Zeno's death, Cleanthes became head of the Stoic school for 32 years and continued to build on his mentor's foundation. Zeno had said that the goal of life was "to live consistently", to which Cleanthes added the words "with nature", reflecting his belief that true freedom comes from humble acceptance of destiny and indifference to material possessions.

Cleanthes' only surviving work, *Hymn to Zeus*, captures the Stoic belief in a rational order governing the universe. In this poem, he reflects on the importance of recognizing the divine intelligence that guides all things, famously declaring, "Lead me on, O Zeus, and thou Destiny, / To that goal long ago to me assigned... / Fate guides the willing, but drags the unwilling."

He died at the age of 99. Cleanthes' pupil, Chrysippus of Soli, would go on to become one of Stoicism's most influential thinkers.

EPICUREANISM

In its early years, Stoicism faced competition from Epicureanism, a school of philosophy founded around 307 BCE. While Stoicism focused on inner peace and advocated virtue as the "highest good" (see p.60), Epicureanism emphasized the pursuit of pleasure and the avoidance of pain as the ultimate goals of life.

Chrysippus of Soli

Following the death of Cleanthes, Chrysippus of Soli headed the school from around 230 until 206 BCE. While Zeno founded the school and Cleanthes nurtured it, it was Chrysippus who transformed Stoicism into a robust, comprehensive philosophy, solidifying its doctrines and ensuring its survival for centuries to come. He is now often considered the true architect of Stoicism.

Chrysippus' achievements are even more impressive given he didn't set out to be a philosopher. Born to a wealthy family in Soli (near present-day Mersin, Turkey), he lost his vast inheritance when it was confiscated by royalty. Much like Cleanthes, who had developed self-discipline and endurance as a boxer, Chrysippus trained as a long-distance runner before turning his focus to intellectual pursuits. His path to Stoicism began when he moved to Athens and encountered the teachings of Cleanthes.

Under Cleanthes' guidance, Chrysippus became deeply immersed in Stoic philosophy, but he wasn't content with merely accepting the ideas passed down to him.

Stoicism for Chrysippus was more than just a way of thinking – it was a way of living and a system that explained not just ethics but the nature of the universe itself. He made significant contributions to the study of knowledge and how we attain it through logic, for example, finding connections and making conclusions.

He also made ethics central to Stoicism. According to Chrysippus, external things like wealth or health may be preferable, but they do not contribute to genuine happiness. Instead, it is our internal moral state, and how we respond to life's challenges, that matters most.

Chrysippus was incredibly prolific, reportedly writing over 700 works, though none have survived. His teachings, preserved through the writings of later Stoics, shaped Stoicism into a concrete philosophical movement and ultimately led to its growth in popularity.

> But for Chrysippus, there had been no Porch.
>
> **Diogenes Laertius,**
> *Lives of Eminent Philosophers*

Diogenes of Babylon

Diogenes of Babylon was born around 230 BCE in Seleucia, Mesopotamia (present-day Iraq), and later moved to Athens, where he became a student of Chrysippus. He eventually rose to leader of the Stoic school and made significant contributions by refining Stoic logic and clarifying how reason should guide actions to align with nature. He argued that our ability to debate rationally, using logic and reason, could help us to understand ourselves and our place in the world.

During his leadership, the Roman Republic began asserting its dominance in the Mediterranean. In 155 BCE, Diogenes was part of a delegation of three competing Athenian philosophers (the others being Carneades the Sceptic and Critolaus the Peripatetic) sent to Rome to protest a hefty fine. While there, he calmly lectured the public, introducing Stoicism to Roman audiences for the first time. His diplomacy convinced the Romans to drop the fine, and his teachings left a lasting impact on Roman thought.

Although Diogenes was a prolific writer, his greatest legacy was bringing Stoicism to Rome, which paved the way for its future dissemination.

Antipater of Tarsus

Antipater of Tarsus, born around 200 BCE in present-day Turkey, was a student of Diogenes of Babylon and later became head of the Stoic school in Athens. Renowned for his sharp intellect, Antipater advanced Stoicism by focusing on practical ethics, logic and active participation in public life. He believed that the wise should engage in society, taking on duties to family, friends and community. He also applied the Stoic concept of living in accordance with nature to both personal and political realms. Though much of his work is lost, Antipater's emphasis on public duty and civic engagement remains central to Stoicism's role as a practical philosophy for life.

ARCHER ANALOGY

Antipater likened Stoic ethics to archery: an archer's attempt to shoot accurately is similar to our efforts, as Stoics, to live good lives. The Stoic focuses on shooting well, but his happiness doesn't depend on whether he hits the target. Success depends on factors beyond our control; what matters is acting virtuously with the right intentions, practising for its own sake and maintaining inner calm regardless of the outcome.

Panaetius of Rhodes

Panaetius of Rhodes, born around 185 BCE, played a pivotal role in bringing Stoicism from Greece to Rome. A student of Diogenes of Babylon and Antipater of Tarsus, he reshaped Stoicism to fit the social and political realities of Roman life.

As a close friend and advisor to Scipio Aemilianus, a Roman general and statesman, Panaetius had direct influence on the Roman aristocracy. Unlike most earlier Stoics, who focused on abstract metaphysics, Panaetius (like Antipater) emphasized practical ethics, making Stoicism more appealing to the Roman elite.

His teachings encouraged active participation in public life, aligning Stoic principles with Roman values of duty and honour. He also softened Stoic views on emotions, arguing that feelings like grief and joy were natural and could be moderated rather than suppressed.

Panaetius' work ensured Stoicism's rise in Roman society, transforming it into a philosophy that guided both personal virtue and public responsibility. He was the last undisputed leader of the Stoic school and died around 110 BCE.

Hecato of Rhodes

Hecato of Rhodes is an often-overlooked but eminent figure of the Middle Stoa period. A student of Panaetius, he expanded on his teacher's Romanized Stoicism, bringing a practical approach to how individuals should live virtuously.

One of Hecato's most notable contributions was his view on wealth. Unlike earlier Stoics, who were indifferent to material possessions, Hecato argued that wealth was acceptable if it was acquired and used virtuously. This view made Stoicism more adaptable to everyday life, balancing moral integrity with practical needs. He also emphasized personal desires and how they could align with virtue, offering a more flexible interpretation of Stoicism. In his *Letters*, Seneca quotes Hecato as saying, "If you want to be loved, love first", which reflects Stoic ideas regarding reciprocity and the power of proactive kindness in building relationships.

Though much of his work is lost (including at least 30 books), Hecato's ideas are preserved through writings by Cicero and Seneca.

Posidonius

Posidonius of Apamea was born around 135 BCE in present-day Syria, into a Greek family. As a young man, he moved to Athens to study under Panaetius. After Panaetius' death around 110 BCE, Posidonius settled in Rhodes and established his own Stoic school.

He developed the Stoic division of philosophy into three fields: physics (including metaphysics and theology), logic (including dialectic) and ethics. For Posidonius, these areas formed a unified whole, with each being essential to the others. He famously likened them to a living body, with physics as flesh and blood, logic as the bones holding everything together and ethics – the most important – as the soul.

Posidonius' influence extended beyond philosophy into many subjects, including mathematics and history. His multi-disciplinary approach helped spread Stoicism across different fields of knowledge, making him a crucial bridge between Greek philosophy and Roman intellectual life. As a prolific writer and traveller, he engaged with the Roman elite, such as Cicero and Pompey, shaping their understanding of Stoicism.

From Greek to Latin

The translation of Stoic teachings from Greek to Latin was a crucial step in spreading Stoicism throughout the Roman world. Marcus Tullius Cicero (106–43 BCE), a respected Roman statesman and philosopher, played a big part in this process. Although not a Stoic himself, Cicero admired Stoicism and incorporated its principles into his own works, helping to introduce Stoic ideas to a Latin audience. His writings, including *Paradoxa Stoicorum* (Stoic Paradoxes) and *De Officiis* (On Duties), distilled Stoic principles in ways that resonated with Roman values of public service and honour.

Known as Rome's greatest orator, Cicero was vital in making Stoicism accessible to the Roman elite, many of whom did not read Greek. Other key figures, such as Panaetius and Posidonius, had already adapted Stoicism to Roman cultural and political life, making it easier for Cicero to translate the philosophy's ideas into the Roman context. Through Cicero's works and speeches, Stoic ethics began to shape Roman law, governance and personal conduct.

Cato the Younger

Marcus Porcius Cato the Younger was a descendant of an old Roman family that had significant political influence. Born in 95 BCE, Cato, in his early years, was educated in the traditional Roman values of duty, discipline and austerity. However, it was Stoicism that left an indelible mark on his character and his career as a statesman. He discovered Stoic philosophy through his tutors, who introduced him to the teachings of philosophers like Zeno and Diogenes of Babylon.

For Cato, Stoicism was more than an intellectual pursuit – it became a code by which he lived. The Stoic ideals of virtue, reason and moral integrity guided his every action, particularly in the chaotic political landscape of the late Roman Republic.

His reputation for incorruptibility and moral courage earned him the respect of many and the enmity of others, including Julius Caesar. Cato's life and actions showed his strong belief in the importance of moral integrity, and, unlike many of his contemporaries, he lived modestly (despite his wealth) and refused to be swayed by bribes or threats, even when it meant personal risk.

One of Cato's most dramatic moments came during the civil war between Pompey and Caesar. He consistently opposed the policies of Caesar, which he saw as tyranny, and chose to fight for the Republic's ideals of liberty and virtue. After Pompey's defeat, Cato chose to take his own life in 46 BCE rather than live under Caesar's government, which he viewed as corrupt. His suicide was a final act of defiance and demonstrated his Stoic adherence to ethical integrity and courage over self-interest.

Cato's commitment to Stoic principles made him a lasting symbol of virtue and moral integrity. His career embodied the Stoic belief that virtue is worth more than wealth, power or even life itself, influencing later Stoic thinkers and shaping Stoicism's legacy in both Roman and modern thought.

> I will begin to speak, when I have that to say which had not better be unsaid.
>
> **Cato the Younger in
> Plutarch's *Parallel Lives***

Gaius Musonius Rufus

Gaius Musonius Rufus was born around 25 CE in Volsinii (thought to be present-day Orvieto, Italy), into a prominent equestrian family, and became one of the most significant Stoic philosophers of his time.

Often called the "Roman Socrates", Musonius was a trailblazer in many ways. He believed that philosophy should not be confined to intellectual debate; it should be a lived experience for everyone, including women. He asserted that both men and women had the same capacity for education and practising virtue and reason. In a society that largely relegated women to the background, this was a revolutionary stance. He also saw marriage and family life as fertile ground for practising the Stoic virtues of patience, endurance and self-control, viewing these relationships as essential to living a virtuous life.

His teachings were rooted in the belief that philosophy was the most useful thing a person could study, as it teaches virtuous action through daily habits and behaviours. Musonius lived by this principle himself. Exiled twice – first by Emperor Nero and later by Vespasian – for his opposition to tyranny and corruption, he continued to teach Stoic ideals wherever he went. Despite his experiences, he suggested tyrants should not be criticized, because "We have the same inclinations as they do; we just lack opportunities to act on them." He saw exile not as a punishment but as a chance to cultivate inner strength, arguing that no one can truly harm you if you master your own mind and live in accordance with virtue. He viewed the discomforts of life not as obstacles to be avoided but as opportunities to strengthen one's character. He advocated:

- Eating modestly to nourish the body, not lavishly for pleasure
- Following an inexpensive, vegetarian diet that is easy to obtain
- Wearing clothes as protection from the elements, not as projections of wealth

Musonius' practical, grounded approach deeply influenced his students, most notably a slave named Epictetus, who was allowed to attend Musonius' lectures (see p.42).

Musonius died sometime before 101–102 CE.

Seneca – early life

Lucius Annaeus Seneca the Younger (better known as Seneca) is one of the most famous and controversial Stoic philosophers. The majority of surviving Stoic writings come from Seneca.

Born around 4 BCE in Corduba, Spain (now Córdoba), Seneca came from a family that was wealthy, educated and influential. His father, Seneca the Elder, was a Spanish-born Roman *equites* (knight) who was also a noted writer and orator, and his mother, Helvia, was known to be highly educated. This meant young Seneca was raised in a privileged environment with access to the finest education of the time.

At the age of five, he was sent to Rome to live with an aunt and receive Roman schooling, which included early exposure to Stoicism and mentorship from philosophers such as Attalus the Stoic and Sotion. These early influences shaped his thinking and the course of his life.

Unfortunately, Seneca suffered a lot of health problems. He struggled with breathing difficulties throughout his life and contracted tuberculosis as a young man. This required him to recuperate in Egypt where, for approximately ten years, his aunt nursed him back to health. In 31 CE, he made the voyage back to Rome with his aunt.

After this ten-year hiatus, Seneca's life as a politician began. He was elected to sit in the Roman Senate, and his oratory skills quickly became legendary. Seneca had a natural ability to captivate an audience; his rhetoric wasn't just flowery language – he wielded Stoic philosophy as a tool for political survival and influence, especially in the volatile and often-treacherous political climate of the Roman Empire. His speeches were persuasive but always tinged with a Stoic detachment, offering the appearance of someone who could advise with cool rationality rather than be swayed by the passions of the Senate.

In 41 CE, during the reign of Emperor Claudius, Seneca was accused of having an affair with Claudius' niece. Although the charge was likely fabricated, it resulted in his exile to the barren island of Corsica. The event coincided with the death of his only son. Seneca spent eight years in Corsica, away from the public eye and cut off from both his wealth and political influence – an experience that became pivotal to his Stoic legacy.

Seneca's legacy

Seneca's exile to Corsica became a period of intellectual growth. He saw exile as an opportunity to apply Stoic philosophy directly to his life – enduring hardship without complaint, focusing on what was within his control and finding meaning in adversity.

His fortunes reversed in 49 CE when he was recalled to Rome by the new empress, Agrippina the Younger, to tutor her son, Nero. This marked the beginning of Seneca's rise to prominence.

When Nero became emperor, Seneca continued to be his advisor and amassed a personal fortune of 300 million sesterces (ancient Roman currency), many villas, vineyards and Egyptian estates (the average Roman senator had about 5 million sesterces). He lent vast amounts of money to indigenous British aristocrats at interest rates that were so exorbitant that when he recalled the loans, he almost crashed the British economy and caused a rebellion.

This wealth became a source of criticism from Seneca's contemporaries and later historians. Many saw a contradiction between his Stoic ideals and his lavish lifestyle. Seneca himself was aware of this tension and, in his writings, he often addressed the complexity of balancing philosophical principles with the realities of life in the political and imperial sphere. He argued that wealth was not inherently evil if used virtuously and not for indulgence.

Seneca's wealth contributed to his eventual downfall, making him a target for suspicion and jealousy at Nero's court, especially as Nero's reign became brutal and erratic. Ultimately, Seneca's wealth and influence could not protect him from Nero's growing paranoia, and he was ordered to commit suicide in 65 CE.

Unlike his Stoic predecessors, who focused on living in accordance with nature, Seneca prioritized role models to "regulate our characters" and be our guides (but not our masters, see p.108). According to Seneca, we should ultimately choose our own path because "The truth lies open to all, it has not yet been taken over." He was widely admired by Romans for his exceptional literary talent, though his political role under Nero compromised his reputation. Despite this, his philosophical works ultimately secured his legacy. For the past two centuries, Seneca's writings, including his *Letters*, have guided countless people and cemented his place as one of the greatest Stoic thinkers in history.

Epictetus – early life

The majority of Stoic philosophers came from wealthy backgrounds and held positions of authority. One of the greatest, however, emerged from the opposite end of the social spectrum: Epictetus. His birth name is lost to history; *epíktētos* in Greek means "gained" or "acquired". Epictetus was born around 55 CE in Hierapolis (in present-day Turkey). The precise date of his arrival in Rome is unknown but he began life there as a slave.

His early years were marked by hardship and severe health issues that left him with a permanent physical disability (he walked with a limp). According to some accounts, this disability may have resulted from the physical abuse of his master.

Despite his physical challenges and the constraints of servitude, Epictetus showed remarkable intellectual ability. He became a servant to Nero's wealthy secretary, Epaphroditus, who allowed him to study philosophy, and he became a student of Musonius Rufus (see p.37). Like Musonius, Epictetus faced immense hardships but did not give in to anger or despair; instead, he went on to become one of the most renowned Stoic philosophers in history. Under Rufus' guidance, Epictetus discovered Stoicism, which would eventually shape his life and legacy. Stoicism not only offered Epictetus a set of beliefs but also a way to transcend his circumstances. The philosophy became a powerful form of resilience for him.

After the death of Emperor Nero, he was granted his freedom and began lecturing with a focus on practical philosophy. Teaching in Rome for over 20 years, he urged students to live in harmony with their nature as rational beings, which he viewed as a gift bestowed by the gods.

Along with other philosophers, he was forced to leave Rome in c.89 CE and eventually settled in Nicopolis, a city in north-western Greece, where he founded a philosophical academy.

THE STOIC OPPOSITION

For much of the first century, Stoic philosophers who openly criticized the tyranny of Roman emperors, such as Nero, Vespasian and Domitian, were persecuted and exiled. Domitian expelled all philosophers from Italy twice (in c.89 CE and 93/94 CE), including Epictetus.

Epictetus' legacy

Epictetus' reputation as a Stoic philosopher grew significantly during his later years in Nicopolis. Unlike many philosophers, who sought fame, Epictetus lived humbly, embodying the Stoic values he taught. His own experiences of suffering and enslavement gave him a unique perspective on the Stoic concept of inner freedom. He believed that true freedom came from within, independent of one's external conditions.

His school quickly gained a good reputation, attracting students from across the Roman Empire. Epictetus emphasized practical philosophy – Stoicism not as an abstract theory but as a guide for daily life. He focused on mastering the mind, accepting fate and aligning one's actions with the rational order of the universe, deeply influencing Roman intellectuals and later Stoic thinkers.

For Epictetus, true courage and strength involved gaining control over one's thoughts and desires, leading to a life guided by ethical principles, regardless of physical limitations or societal status.

Epictetus taught Stoicism until his death around 135 CE (at the age of about 80). He left an enduring legacy in Stoic philosophy, despite never writing any books or publishing works himself. His profound teachings on ethics, resilience and personal freedom were preserved by his most famous student, Arrian of Nicomedia, who transcribed them in *The Discourses of Epictetus* and the much-loved *Enchiridion* (or Handbook). Through these works (which concentrate almost exclusively on ethics), Epictetus' ideas on controlling what lies within our power, while accepting what is beyond our control, have influenced countless thinkers. Centuries after his death, his emphasis on inner strength and rational living continues to inspire individuals to embrace Stoicism as a practical guide to life.

> To make the best of what is in our power,
> and take the rest as it occurs.
>
> **Epictetus, in *Discourses***

Marcus Aurelius – early life

Marcus Aurelius, often hailed as the "Philosopher King", stands out in history as a rare blend of power and wisdom. As one of Rome's most prominent leaders, he wielded immense authority while remaining loyal to Stoic philosophy.

Born in Rome in 121 CE, Marcus came from a wealthy and influential family. His father, Marcus Annius Verus, was a prominent senator, and his mother, Domitia Lucilla, inherited vast estates. His aunt was married to the man who was destined to become the next emperor (Antoninus Pius), whom he would eventually succeed.

After his father's death when Marcus was three, he was raised primarily by his grandfather and developed a deep sense of duty and responsibility towards Rome. Even in his early years, he showed an unusual interest in philosophy rather than the comforts of aristocratic life. One of his teachers, Diognetus, a painting master, introduced Marcus to the philosophic way of life. Around the age of 11, he started adopting habits common to philosophers at the time: he studied while wearing a rough Greek cloak and slept on the ground until his mother persuaded him to sleep on a bed. He favoured a life of discipline and contemplation over the indulgences of aristocratic privilege.

Following a directive from Emperor Hadrian, Marcus was adopted by Antoninus Pius. In 161 CE, at the age of 39, he succeeded Antoninus as emperor, ruling jointly with Lucius Verus (another adopted son of Antoninus). Despite their shared rule, Marcus was the more influential and respected of the two emperors.

"FIVE GOOD EMPERORS"

The "Five Good Emperors" were a line of Roman rulers – Nerva, Trajan, Hadrian, Antoninus Pius and Marcus Aurelius – who brought stability and prosperity to the Roman Empire from 96 to 180 CE. They selected and adopted capable heirs based on merit and values, ensuring smooth transitions of power.

Marcus Aurelius' legacy

From 161 until his death in 180 CE, Marcus Aurelius ruled as Roman emperor, guiding the empire through one of its most turbulent times. Faced with a devastating plague, which claimed ten per cent of the population, and two major wars, Marcus held the empire together while maintaining his reputation as a popular and respected leader.

His collection of writings, known today as *Meditations*, is one of the most important works of Stoic philosophy. Mostly written during his military campaign in central Europe, the writings reflect the intense challenges he faced as emperor and military commander. Harsh battlefield conditions, ongoing wars and profound personal grief (including for the deaths of many of his children) provided the backdrop for some of his reflections on hardship, duty and mortality.

Marcus' choice to write in Greek reflects his deep connection to Stoicism. Greek was the language of philosophy in the ancient world, especially for the Stoics. By choosing Greek, Marcus associated himself with this tradition, emphasizing his philosophical identity over his political role as emperor of Rome, where Latin was dominant.

The simplicity and directness of his language also reflect Stoic ideals of clarity, self-discipline and rationality. Stoicism values clear thinking and communication, free from unnecessary flourishes or emotional excess. The mix of clarity and brutal honesty makes *Meditations* not only a cornerstone of Stoic philosophy but also a truly remarkable and unique text in the history of human thought. It reveals an emperor reminding himself to stay grounded, to avoid being corrupted by luxury and to meet every challenge with resilience and reason. What makes it even more extraordinary is that it was never intended for public view – it was Marcus' private journal, a personal space where he wrestled with his own thoughts and challenges. The survival of these raw, intimate reflections from one of history's most powerful leaders has been deeply valued by subsequent philosophers.

Ambition means tying your well-being
to what other people say or do... Sanity
means tying it to your own actions.

Marcus Aurelius, *Meditations*

After Marcus Aurelius

After Marcus Aurelius' death, Christianity gradually rose to dominate the Roman world, reshaping moral thought and sidelining many of the ancient schools of philosophy – including Stoicism. During the Renaissance, it made a brief yet fascinating comeback thanks to Justus Lipsius (1547–1606). He sought to revive Stoic ideals of self-control and virtue by blending them with Christian teachings. His movement, known as Neo-Stoicism, aimed to show that Stoic principles could coexist with Christian faith.

Though Neo-Stoicism didn't last long, its impact can be traced through some of the greatest minds of the seventeenth century. Philosophers such as René Descartes (1596–1650) and Baruch Spinoza (1632–1677) were influenced by Stoic ideas – Spinoza, in particular, echoed the Stoic belief in rationality and emotional mastery in his work.

While Stoicism faded from mainstream thought, its core ideas – living with virtue, controlling one's emotions and focusing on what is within our control – quietly influenced thinkers such as Immanuel Kant (1724–1804), whose ideas on duty echo Stoic ethics, and John Stuart Mill (1806–1873), who admired Stoic resilience. These philosophical threads paved the way for Stoicism's modern revival.

STOIC
PHILOSOPHY
AND THE
FOUR VIRTUES

Now that you're familiar with the lives and teachings of key Stoic philosophers, it's time to delve deeper into Stoicism's core principles. More than just an abstract set of ideas, Stoicism offers a practical approach to navigating life's challenges.

This chapter explores the beliefs, values and principles that form the foundation of Stoic philosophy. You'll look at:

- ◆ The Four Virtues – wisdom, courage, temperance and justice
- ◆ Epistemology – the study of knowledge and reason
- ◆ Stoic ethics – how they guide moral decisions
- ◆ Passions – Stoic views on managing passions or emotions

At its core, Stoicism teaches that true happiness doesn't come from external circumstances but from cultivating inner virtue and wisdom. The Stoics emphasize focusing on what we can control – our thoughts, actions and reactions – while calmly accepting the things beyond our power.

A complete system

The philosophers of the Early Stoa (see p.20), led by figures like Zeno and Chrysippus, developed a remarkably comprehensive philosophical system that intertwined logic, ethics and physics. Unlike modern philosophy, where these fields are often separated, the ancient Stoics viewed them as interconnected parts of a unified whole. For Zeno, logic included subjects like epistemology and language, enabling the wise to discern truth from falsehood.

Stoic physics was more of a philosophy of nature than what we think of as physics today. Zeno believed the universe operated in cycles governed by a divine rationality. He introduced the concept of a "divine fire", a pure and fundamental element that gave rise to the cosmos and which organizes everything in it, with God or Zeus representing this universal rational force.

Chrysippus expanded these ideas, arguing that logic, ethics and physics must be understood together. The ancient Stoics believed that understanding how the universe works (physics) and how we can know it (logic) were essential to living virtuously (ethics), creating a cohesive system of thought for navigating life.

Logic and physics

HOW TO THINK

The Early Stoa philosophers crafted a unique vision of logic and physics, seeing them as interconnected disciplines that offered a deeper understanding of the universe. For them, logic was more than a set of rules for formal reasoning; it was the key to understanding how to think and communicate clearly. It helped people to grasp the nature of truth, distinguishing between what is real and what is false. This ability to reason was central to living in harmony with the universe.

Stoic physics examined the nature of reality and the structure of the universe. The Stoics taught that the cosmos was a single, rational entity guided by a divine, orderly force. Everything on Earth, from the changing seasons to the moon's cycles and the tides, is interconnected, following a harmonious, rational order. By adopting habits like regular reflection (see p.73) and rest breaks (see p.95), they believed that humans, as an integral part of this whole, could align their actions with this natural harmony.

For the early Stoics, logic and physics together formed the foundation for Stoic ethics, shaping how individuals understood the world and how they should live within it.

> They liken Philosophy to a fertile field:
> Logic being the encircling fence, Ethics the crop, Physics the soil or the trees.
>
> **Diogenes Laertius,**
> *Lives of Eminent Philosophers*

HOW TO LIVE

According to the surviving texts, the late Stoics mostly set aside technical discussions of physics and logic and focused their attention on practical ethics as the path to *eudaimonia* – the ultimate goal of Stoic life. Thinkers like Seneca, Epictetus and Marcus Aurelius emphasized how to live virtuously in everyday life. This shift was nevertheless still rooted in the idea of living in harmony with the rational, interconnected structure of the world, which they believed could only be achieved through wisdom and logic.

Eudaimonia

Eudaimonia is often translated as "the flourishing life" or "a well-lived life". For the Stoics, this wasn't simply about feeling happy but about achieving deep contentment through making virtuous choices and the thoughtful use of our uniquely human capacity for reason. In early Stoicism, the idea of *eudaimonia* was tied to the Stoics' holistic view of philosophy. Each part – logic, physics and ethics – was essential to living well. Achieving *eudaimonia*, therefore, meant understanding the universe through logic and physics and applying that knowledge to live virtuously.

As Stoicism evolved, this focus on virtue became more central. Later Stoics, such as Epictetus and Marcus Aurelius, emphasized that while we can't control external events, living with integrity and making principled choices were the key to *eudaimonia*. For them, aligning with the natural order of the universe meant cultivating wisdom, courage, justice and temperance, which would lead to lasting fulfilment even in the face of life's challenges.

For Socrates and the Stoics, a *eudaimonic* life meant acting in the right way. They believed evil is not done willingly or knowingly but because of *amathia*, meaning moral ignorance or lack of wisdom.

Ethics

Ethics became the heart of the philosophy during the first and second centuries CE. While early Stoics emphasized a balanced system of logic, physics and ethics, Roman Stoics like Seneca and Epictetus focused primarily on practical ethics, which they viewed as essential to everyday life.

For the Stoics, a "good life" was not defined by external circumstances (such as health or reputation) but by the quality of one's moral choices. They believed that living with dignity and fulfilling the natural human drive for connection, cooperation and generosity constituted a life well lived. Each of the virtues they identified (see p.61) played a critical role in ethical living.

By accepting that things like wealth or place of birth are beyond our control, we can focus our attention on our actions and responses. Cultivating a virtuous character through this mindset was, for the Stoics, the path to *eudaimonia*.

> Over a man who is wise, chance has little power.
>
> **Epicurus, in Cicero's *On The Good Life***

Indifferents

In Stoicism, a person's external circumstances, such as wealth, appearance or power, are referred to as *ta adiaphora* – meaning "indifferents" or "indifferent things". This has often led to Stoicism being misunderstood as an encouragement to be completely indifferent to external circumstances (such as poverty or illness), which is an incorrect interpretation.

The idea that all external things are entirely indifferent is closer to the beliefs of Cynics, Sceptics or Aristo of Chios, a contemporary of Zeno who took the absolutist view that everything other than virtue and vice should be viewed with indifference. For those philosophers, everything outside virtue and vice – things like health, wealth, property or reputation – was deemed indifferent because they were external to our moral choices.

However, Zeno, the founder of Stoicism, distinguished his school of thought by introducing a more nuanced approach. While externals are indifferent in the sense that they don't *determine* virtue, Stoics recognized that some externals still have value. Epictetus explained that only our actions can be truly good or bad, while everything else lies outside our moral control. This is where the concept of "preferred" and "dispreferred indifferents" comes in:

- ◆ "Preferred indifferents" (*ta proêgmena*) – They're not inherently good but should be pursued in line with virtue: things like health, beauty, wealth, strength and reputation. These are in keeping with human nature and help us to practise virtue.
- ◆ "Dispreferred indifferents" (*ta aproêgmena*) – They should be avoided if possible because they detract from our ability to live well and fulfil our natural potential: illness/pain, poverty, ignoble birth, low reputation or social exclusion. If unavoidable, enduring them with virtue is key to living a Stoic life.

This subtle distinction allowed Stoics to live practically, balancing their pursuit of virtue with life's inevitable challenges.

> You are not your body and hairstyle, but your capacity for choosing well. If your choices are beautiful, so too will you be.
>
> **Epictetus, in *Discourses***

Virtue

The concept of virtue was common in Ancient Greek philosophy, with early thinkers like Socrates viewing it as essential to happiness and well-being. Aristotle distinguished between *intellectual* virtue (such as understanding and wisdom), developed through instruction and learning, and *moral* virtue (such as temperance and bravery), cultivated through habit and practice. The earliest Stoics built on these ideas but placed virtue at the very heart of the philosophy. For Chrysippus, living a virtuous life meant practising good habits and consistently choosing actions guided by reason. The Stoics believed that virtue, rather than wealth or pleasure, was the ultimate aim in life – the *summum bonum*, or "highest good".

DEFINING EXCELLENCE

A Greek philosophical dictionary titled *Definitions* from the time of Plato defined *areté* (virtue/excellence) as "The best disposition; the state of a mortal creature which is in itself praiseworthy... he who is so disposed is said to be perfectly excellent."

The cardinal virtues

The Stoics adapted ancient philosophical ideas about virtue to reflect their belief that living in accordance with nature and reason guides you towards *eudaimonia* – a well-lived, fulfilling life. They adopted Socrates' division of four aspects of virtue and defined them as follows:

- **Wisdom** (or prudence) – Seeking truth and making thoughtful decisions. Identifying what's within your control and what is not, so you can navigate life with clarity and purpose.
- **Courage** – Being consistent, compassionate and vulnerable. Whether it's standing up for your principles or pushing through difficult times, courage helps you to act wisely.
- **Temperance** – Practising self-control and moderation. This means resisting excessive behaviour, such as overspending or overeating, and controlling your desires.
- **Justice** – Treating others fairly. A just society depends on respect, empathy and ensuring everyone is treated with dignity.

Wisdom

The Stoic virtue of wisdom, or *phronesis*, is all about practical knowledge – knowing how to live well and make sound decisions. For the Stoics, wisdom wasn't just an abstract idea; it was the ability to judge what is truly valuable in life and what determines our actions and inactions. It's wisdom that informs our application of the other three cardinal virtues of courage, temperance and justice.

At its core, wisdom means recognizing the "dichotomy of control": understanding what is within our control (such as our actions, beliefs and desires) and what is not (such as external events or other people's opinions). By focusing on what we can control, we can use wisdom to help us to lead a virtuous life. For the Stoics, this internal clarity far outweighed the pursuit of externals like material gain, wealth, reputation and status.

Epictetus often reminded his students that we cannot change external events, but we can change how we think about them. For example, if someone insults you, a wise response would be to recognize that their words are beyond your control and that only your reaction matters.

This shift in thinking is wisdom in action – recognizing what you can't change and choosing how to respond. Marcus Aurelius, in *Meditations*, frequently wrote about using wisdom to remain calm and logical, even in the face of adversity, recognizing that the universe has its own natural order beyond our influence.

In Stoicism, wisdom isn't just about knowledge – it's the practical art of living well, of knowing when to act and when to let go. By applying wisdom, you learn to navigate challenges with a clear, rational mindset, improving both your mental state and your ability to thrive in everyday situations.

> If a person gave away your body to some passerby, you'd be furious. Yet you hand over your mind to anyone who comes along... leaving it disturbed and troubled – have you no shame in that?
>
> **Epictetus, in *Enchiridion***

True knowledge

The Stoics believed that true knowledge wasn't just about having accurate beliefs – it required absolute certainty. For them, knowledge (*epistêmê*) was the pinnacle of intellectual achievement built on unshakeable foundations. But how do we get there? That's where Stoic epistemology comes in.

At the heart of their theory is the concept of *katalepsis*, or "grasping". The Stoics defined a "graspable presentation" (*phantasia kataléptikê*) as one so clear and distinct that it couldn't logically be doubted, such as recognizing a friend's face or knowing you're seeing a solid object, like a tree. Sensory impressions give us direct access to the world, such as feeling rain on our skin, while thought processes reveal non-sensory ones, like understanding that kindness builds trust or reasoning that tomorrow's sunrise is inevitable. However, impressions alone aren't enough; it's how we respond to them that matters.

When an impression arises (a feeling, perception or idea), it's up to us to judge its truth. While we can't control the impressions we receive (they come from external forces), we have full control over how we handle them. This response involves carefully evaluating whether the impression is true or false. By practising thoughtful judgement, we can choose to react in a way that respects Stoic values, regardless of any external circumstances.

Knowledge is, therefore, not simply holding a true belief but grasping it so firmly that no argument or doubt can dislodge it.

Zeno of Citium used a vivid analogy to explain this. Holding out an open hand, he said, "This is what a presentation is like." Closing his fingers symbolized accepting the impression as truth. Making a fist showed a stronger commitment; it represented firmly held knowledge. Finally, by covering the fist with his other hand, he illustrated unshakeable certainty. This was a level of certainty that was rare and reserved for the sage – a model of perfect wisdom.

The Stoics acknowledged that most of us navigate life with beliefs and opinions that lack such solidity. Despite it being difficult for us to achieve true knowledge, Stoic epistemology urges us to think critically and question deeply, always striving for intellectual rigour and clarity.

> How satisfying it is to dismiss and block out any upsetting or foreign impression, and immediately to have peace in all things.
>
> **Marcus Aurelius, *Meditations***

The soul

The foundation of Stoic ethics lies in the belief that true good resides in the state of the soul (*psuchê*). The Stoics taught that the soul is a "corporeal" substance, a physical part of us, and even a fragment of the divine – an aspect of God that animates our bodies and grants us reason and intelligence. They viewed the soul as both rational and divine, intrinsically connected to the universe's natural order. Wisdom, accordingly, is the soul's ability to align with reason, helping it to transcend distractions like desires, fears and external events.

By cultivating wisdom, people nurture this rational part of the soul, enabling them to distinguish between what is within their control and what is not. A soul guided by wisdom remains focused on its internal state rather than being swayed by external circumstances.

The Stoics believed that the soul's highest function is to exercise sound judgement, which leads to virtuous actions. They viewed the divine and rational aspect of the soul, called the *daimon*, as a guardian or inner genius that helps individuals live in agreement with nature. By achieving this harmony, the soul works in parallel with the divine order of the *logos*. Marcus Aurelius frequently wrote about keeping his *daimon* pure to prevent his soul from becoming "an abscess and a sort of morbid outgrowth on the universe". Similarly, Epictetus emphasized that true power lies within our soul, not in the outside world. By nurturing wisdom, the soul grows resilient, allowing us to face life's challenges with inner peace and avoid unnecessary distress.

A VITAL FORCE

In Stoic physics, *pneuma* is a central concept representing the "breath of life", a blend of the elements of air and fire. The air symbolizes motion, while the fire signifies warmth, together creating the vital force that binds the cosmos and everything in it together, including every individual. The cosmos is, therefore, a single continuum of *pneuma*-charged substance. In its highest form, *pneuma* is the human soul, which is a fragment of the soul of the deity.

Reason

In Stoicism, reason (*logos*) is central to understanding the universe and guiding human behaviour (see p.10). The Stoics believed that reason was not just a human faculty but a divine element, a part of the universal order that pervades everything. For them, to live according to reason was to live in harmony with nature, as reason and the natural world were seen as intertwined. The Stoic virtue of wisdom stems directly from this belief in the power of reason.

Stoics like Chrysippus and Epictetus taught that reason is the guiding force for ethical – in other words, virtuous – decision-making. Chrysippus believed that every human has the capacity for rational thought, and it is through the proper use of this capacity that we can achieve wisdom and lead a virtuous life.

According to Epictetus, when we face challenges or difficulties, reason helps us focus on what truly matters – our actions, decisions and character – while helping us detach from the external world, which is beyond our control. In discussing this choice we all face, he said, "You must diligently work either on your own reasoning or on things out of your control – take great care with the inside and not what's outside", emphasizing that reason helps us respond calmly to life's ups and downs.

Seneca also stressed the importance of reason in his *Letters*. He argued that "burdensome things can be made to press less severely on those who bear them cleverly". For Seneca, wisdom meant understanding that our emotions often cloud judgement, but through reason, we can control them and act virtuously.

Passions

The Stoics believed that to live a virtuous life, one must strive to be free from harmful passions. However, the Stoic concept of "passions" (*pathē*) refers to emotional *disturbances* rather than emotions in general. They believed passions were irrational impulses caused by false opinions or mistaken thinking about the value of something; they're essentially errors in judgement. Therefore, mastering one's passions was not about suppressing emotion entirely but learning to distinguish between rational and irrational emotional responses.

The Stoics identified four primary passions we should strive to avoid:

- **Distress** – envy, anxiety, grief
- **Delight** – malice, indulgence
- **Fear** – cowardice, shame
- **Lust** – anger, greed, craving

These passions arise when we mistake external things – such as wealth, status or reputation – for true goods, leading us to react emotionally when we fear losing them or fail to attain them. The Stoic virtue of wisdom is crucial here because it enables us to see through these negative emotional reactions and focus on what truly matters – our own rational actions and moral character.

Seneca and Epictetus offered practical advice on how to deal with passions. Seneca, in his *Letters*, argued that passions are like a storm that disturbs the mind, and reason is the anchor that holds it steady. He believed that by exercising rational control over our emotions, we can free ourselves from the disturbances caused by passions. Epictetus, on the other hand, taught that we must train ourselves to view external events with detachment through practices like daily self-reflection and journalling. For example, if we lose a valued possession or face a difficult situation, instead of reacting with anger or distress, we should use wisdom to exercise rational thinking and accept that some things are beyond our control.

Ultimately, the Stoic path to wisdom involves transforming passions into rational, controlled responses. By doing so, we achieve emotional resilience and inner peace – hallmarks of a truly wise person.

Inborn tools

Stoicism teaches that human beings are an integral part of nature and are naturally equipped with the tools needed to navigate life's challenges. By understanding and using these innate abilities, we can lead lives that are both virtuous and deeply fulfilling.

Zeno believed that each of us has a *daimon*, an inner genius or purpose, that connects us to the universal nature. Panaetius thought that humans are born with innate virtues and an instinct to use them; we can all thrive and live nobly if we learn to live consistently with our own nature and our duties while maximizing the resources given to us. Marcus Aurelius often reflected on the idea of nature as a guiding force. He believed that by accepting nature's cycles – birth, growth, decay and death – humans could achieve inner peace. Epictetus also stressed the importance of accepting what nature provides (including our senses, reason and power of choice), arguing that much of our distress comes from resisting the natural flow of life.

By using these inborn skills, including our ability to reason, we can accept life's challenges and identify ways to overcome them.

Self-reflection

Journalling is a well-known practice today for self-improvement, but the tradition of moral self-examination is deeply rooted in Stoicism. The Stoics taught that self-reflection is essential to cultivating wisdom. By regularly examining one's actions, thoughts and emotions, Stoics believed that individuals could identify where they were falling short and where they could improve, thereby aligning more closely with virtue.

Marcus Aurelius' *Meditations* is a prime example; he used journalling to remind himself of Stoic principles, to evaluate his thoughts and actions and as a tool to stay mindful of his pursuit of wisdom and integrity. Epictetus and Seneca, too, advised individuals to review their day each evening, to assess whether they had lived according to their principles.

This practice also touches on the idea of *premeditatio malorum* (premeditation of evils, see p.82). The ancient Stoics believed that visualizing negative events, such as becoming homeless or grieving a friend, can help you to be grateful for the people and privileges you have, while reminding you of life's impermanence.

Courage

The Stoic virtue of courage, or *andreia* in Greek, is central to living a life of wisdom and integrity. Courage for the Stoics wasn't just about physical bravery but also, more importantly, about moral courage – the ability to face adversity, fear and hardship with calmness and reason. It's the strength to act in accordance with virtue, even when circumstances are difficult or uncertain.

In Stoic terms, courage means standing firm in the face of life's inevitable challenges, whether they come in the form of illness, loss or social pressure. Epictetus, for example, often reminded his students that we cannot control external events, only how we respond to them. He emphasized that true courage comes from accepting what we cannot change and focusing on maintaining our virtue despite external obstacles. As he famously said, "It is not what happens to you, but how you react to it that matters." This highlights the Stoic idea that courage is about controlling one's inner state, not seeking danger or discomfort.

Seneca also saw courage as integral to Stoicism, particularly in facing life's hardships with dignity. He wrote about the importance of mental fortitude in the face of pain, poverty or death. According to Seneca, to live a virtuous life, one must be prepared to endure suffering with resilience and grace.

Perhaps the best-known example of Stoic courage comes from Marcus Aurelius. As both a philosopher and emperor, he faced immense pressures, including war, political strife and personal loss. Yet, *Meditations* reveals a man determined to remain courageous in the face of these adversities. He reminds himself to "be like the rock that the waves keep crashing over"; this rock "stands unmoved and the raging of the sea falls still around it".

In everyday life, Stoic courage tells us to confront our fears, face difficult truths and maintain our integrity, no matter how tough the situation. It's not just about boldness in action but also about consistency in character, guided by reason and virtue in every circumstance.

> The Stoics, therefore, correctly define courage as "that virtue which champions the cause of right".
>
> **Cicero, *On Duties***

Obstacles and endurance

The Stoics did not view courage as a call to recklessness or impulsive action; instead, courage was the ability to remain upright and composed through life's difficulties without losing moral integrity. Endurance was a key aspect of this definition. Life, they believed, inevitably brings problems – physical pain, emotional distress or unforeseen hardships. The proactive and intentional practice of facing these challenges with dignity and strength reflects our character.

The Stoics taught that obstacles were not merely challenges to overcome – they were opportunities for the growth and cultivation of virtue, particularly courage. By encountering obstacles, we develop courage – the ability to persevere in the face of fear, hardship and uncertainty. Marcus Aurelius exemplified this outlook in his writing when he pondered how to remain calm and clear-headed in the face of adversity. As he famously wrote in *Meditations*, "The impediment to action advances action. What stands in the way becomes the way." This reflects the Stoic mindset that adversity can be transformed into fuel for progress.

In a separate passage, he says, "Receive without pride, let go without attachment." For Marcus, this attitude fosters resilience and courage by teaching us to endure life's challenges with serenity. By keeping emotions in check and applying reason, he believed we could act wisely, preserving inner peace despite external turmoil.

For Epictetus, endurance of life's obstacles was about accepting discomfort and hardship as opportunities to build inner strength. Seneca, too, emphasized that life's difficulties were not to be feared but welcomed as a test of one's inner strength. When he was exiled to the island of Corsica on charges of adultery, a severe punishment that left him isolated and cut off from Roman society, he did not succumb to bitterness. He used this period to reflect, write and deepen his philosophical understanding. In his *Letters*, he wrote, "Difficulties strengthen the mind, as labour does the body", and "misfortune is virtue's opportunity".

This reframing of challenges as opportunities allowed Stoics to face adversity with resilience, viewing each obstacle as a chance to build a stronger, more virtuous self.

Persist and resist

Epictetus' maxim "persist and resist" represents a fundamental Stoic teaching that embodies the virtue of courage. To persist means to continue striving for virtuous living, even when life becomes difficult, while to resist means standing firm against the temptations and distractions that lead us away from wisdom and virtue. Together, these principles form a powerful guide for navigating life's challenges with resilience.

For the Stoics, courage was not just about facing external dangers; it was about enduring internal struggles as well. As Epictetus' advice is sometimes translated, "endure and renounce" – endure hardships; renounce distractions and harmful desires. This meant pushing forwards despite fatigue, fear or adversity and resisting the pull of anger, distress and pleasure, which could lead us astray. It is a process of building inner strength and fortitude grounded in the belief that we can control our responses even when we cannot control the circumstances.

Marcus Aurelius, in *Meditations*, encouraged the practice of persistence by reminding himself daily to accept what happens and to endure whatever life throws at him: "If it is endurable, then endure it. Stop complaining." He saw life's challenges as opportunities to exercise resilience, using the Stoic motto of "persist and resist" to maintain a steady mind.

The Stoics also taught that resisting temptation or the influence of negative emotions was crucial to maintaining a virtuous life. Seneca discussed the importance of resisting the "tyranny of passion", believing that to give in to anger, fear or grief was to surrender one's freedom.

By persisting through hardships and resisting harmful influences, Stoics believed one could cultivate the courage necessary to live a virtuous and fulfilling life. It's not about avoiding difficulties but using them as a means to grow stronger and wiser.

> There are two vices much blacker and more serious than the rest: lack of persistence and lack of self-control.
>
> **Epictetus, in Aulus Gellius' *Attic Nights***

Vulnerability

In the twenty-first century, the term vulnerability often refers to emotional openness and the courage to face uncertainty. While the word isn't commonly associated with ancient Stoics, they nevertheless emphasized similar ideas, valuing the recognition of human limitations, the acceptance of challenges and the understanding of our interconnectedness. These qualities were integral to the virtue of courage. The Stoics believed that acknowledging our weaknesses allows us to confront our fears and act in line with our values. True bravery involves facing discomfort and uncertainty while remaining steadfast in our principles.

Stoic courage is not just about bold actions, therefore, but also about embracing vulnerability by being authentic and truthful, even at great personal risk. Musonius Rufus demonstrated this when he criticized political corruption and moral failings, openly rebuking Nero's oppressive rule. His willingness to speak out, knowing it could lead to exile or worse, shows how vulnerability can build our integrity and resilience.

By embracing our vulnerabilities, we can resist the urge to conform or act dishonestly.

Voluntary discomfort

The Stoic principle of voluntary discomfort involves intentionally exposing oneself to hardships to build resilience and cultivate the virtue of courage. The Stoics believed that by practising discomfort – such as fasting, sleeping on the ground or enduring cold weather – we strengthen our ability to tolerate adversity and develop a mindset that's less dependent on external comforts. This practice prepares us to face life's inevitable challenges with greater composure and inner strength.

For instance, Seneca (one of the wealthiest people of his time) often practised voluntary discomfort by avoiding luxury, believing it helped him gain control over his desires. He wrote, "Set aside a certain number of days, during which you shall be content with the scantiest and cheapest fare... saying to yourself the while: 'Is this the condition that I feared?'"

By choosing discomfort voluntarily, Stoics could practise courage in small, controlled ways, reinforcing the idea that external circumstances don't define us.

Premeditatio malorum

The Stoic practice of *premeditatio malorum*, or "premeditation of evils", is a mental exercise in imagining potential setbacks or hardships before they happen. This practice was seen as vital to the Stoic virtue of wisdom, as it prepares the mind to face difficulties with reason and composure. Seneca wrote extensively on this, suggesting we should visualize possible losses – of wealth, status or loved ones – not to breed fear but to strengthen resilience. By imagining adversity, we train ourselves to respond calmly, reducing the shock and emotional turmoil when challenges arise.

Marcus Aurelius also used this approach. In *Meditations*, he reflected on the fleeting nature of life and the inevitability of hardship, reminding himself that anticipating trials made him better equipped to accept them wisely. Through *premeditatio malorum*, Stoics aimed to gain a realistic understanding of life, enhancing their capacity for reasoned decision-making in the face of adversity.

Reflect on mortality

Memento mori, a Latin phrase meaning "remember you must die", is a powerful concept embedded in the Stoic practice of *premeditatio malorum*, reminding us of life's brevity and the certainty of death. The phrase is believed to have originated from an ancient Roman tradition: after a victory, a servant would whisper the phrase in the ear of the victorious general during his triumphal procession in. The concept was embraced by many ancient philosophers, including Socrates, who said that philosophy is "about nothing else but dying and being dead".

The Stoics believed that regularly contemplating mortality enables us to approach life with greater purpose and presence. This practice, like *premeditatio malorum*, is not about fostering fear but about developing courage and a balanced perspective in the face of life's impermanence.

Seneca believed that by acknowledging death's inevitability, we can overcome the anxiety it often brings, allowing us to live fully and without hesitation. For Marcus Aurelius, reflecting on mortality reminded him not to waste time on meaningless pursuits.

Heroic acceptance

The ancient Stoics believed deeply in accepting personal limitations and trusting in natural providence, which they saw as an expression of divine will. The Stoics believed that every event in the cosmos was fated and determined to occur. This perspective is encapsulated in the Latin phrase *amor fati* (love of fate) – the concept of fully embracing one's fate and finding value, even joy, in all experiences, whether pleasant or difficult. Such acceptance aligns with the Stoic principle of living in harmony with nature: welcoming events as they unfold as parts of a vast, rational order.

For Stoics like Epictetus, wisdom is grounded in the understanding that, while we cannot control external events, we are responsible for our responses. By accepting fate without resistance, one nurtures a peaceful, resilient mind. Marcus Aurelius expressed this in *Meditations*, urging himself to "accept the things to which fate binds you and love the people with whom fate brings you together, but do so with all your heart." To him, each occurrence was part of a greater, interconnected universe.

Mindfulness

The Stoics held mindfulness as an essential practice, believing that wisdom comes from focusing on the present moment rather than getting lost in hypothetical fears about the future. They taught that by staying fully engaged with the current moment, we develop clarity and resilience, making us able to respond wisely to life's challenges as they unfold. Marcus Aurelius wrote, "Your mind will take the shape of what you frequently hold in thought, for the human spirit is coloured by such impressions." He believed that fixating on anxious thoughts about the future disrupts the mind's natural tranquillity, leading to unnecessary stress.

Epictetus also emphasized this idea, encouraging his students to focus their attention on what is within their immediate control. By dealing with each moment on its own terms, he argued, we can remain calm and act thoughtfully rather than reacting impulsively out of fear. In this way, mindfulness supports the Stoic pursuit of courage, grounding us in the present and allowing for a reasoned, purposeful response to life's ever-changing circumstances.

Temperance

The Stoic virtue of temperance, or self-control, is central to the philosophy, guiding people to manage their desires and impulses in pursuit of a balanced, meaningful life. For the Stoics, temperance is not about strict abstinence or the suppression of all pleasures; rather, it's about moderation and restraint, choosing actions that mirror one's values and lead to a harmonious life. This form of self-control helps individuals focus on what truly matters, avoiding excesses that can lead to distraction, dependency or regret.

Seneca frequently addressed the importance of temperance, describing it as the ability to enjoy life's pleasures without being dominated by them. He cautioned against becoming enslaved to fleeting desires or passions, which he believed could weaken a person's character. Instead, he encouraged people to find satisfaction in moderation, teaching that temperance fosters inner freedom and stability. "Drunkenness does not create vices," he wrote, "but it brings them out." For Seneca, temperance allowed people to act from reason rather than impulse, preserving the integrity of the mind.

Epictetus also saw temperance as crucial to self-mastery. He argued that external pleasures, when indulged excessively, could distract from one's higher purpose. Epictetus taught that a person who practises temperance gains a kind of inner independence, since they are less vulnerable to being "tossed about" by external events or desires. His advice to students was to examine their responses to pleasure and to be mindful of the motivations behind their actions. By practising self-restraint, he said, people could cultivate a steady, focused mind that wasn't easily thrown off course by temptation.

Marcus Aurelius urged himself to "be free of passion and yet full of love". He saw temperance as a way to interact meaningfully with others, balancing emotions to act in accordance with reason and empathy. Temperance, he believed, allowed him to respond wisely rather than react impulsively, especially to the pressures of his role as emperor.

Three disciplines

Epictetus outlined three practical disciplines, or areas of self-control, as central to Stoic practice: desire, action and assent. These disciplines work together to promote a balanced life, guiding us to manage our emotions, regulate our responses and develop the other cardinal virtues in the following ways.

DISCIPLINE OF DESIRE (*OREXIS*)

Stoic acceptance, derived from physics (also relates to courage)
This discipline teaches us to manage our impulses by focusing only on what is within our control, such as our choices, judgements and attitudes. We should desire only what aligns with our values and let go of attachment to external outcomes – things we cannot control, like others' opinions or life events. This discipline encourages us to moderate our desires, helping us avoid excessive cravings or dependency, which are obstacles to true freedom and peace. By restraining our desires, we practise temperance, choosing wisely what to pursue and what to let go.

DISCIPLINE OF ACTION (*HORMÊ*)

Stoic philanthropy, derived from ethics (also relates to justice)

This discipline addresses how we conduct ourselves in daily life. Epictetus urged Stoics to act in accordance with reason and virtue, whereby our actions demonstrate our principles rather than succumbing to fleeting emotions or societal pressures. Practising temperance in our actions means exercising restraint, behaving thoughtfully and avoiding impulsive reactions. Through temperance, we can act consistently with our values, maintaining our integrity regardless of external circumstances.

DISCIPLINE OF ASSENT (*SUNKATATHESIS*)

Stoic mindfulness, derived from logic (also relates to wisdom)

This discipline involves managing our reactions to thoughts and impressions. Epictetus believed that the mind's judgements shape our emotions and actions. To practise this discipline, we must evaluate our impressions carefully, deciding which are worth accepting and which are best dismissed. By tempering our judgements, we avoid overreacting or becoming swept up by unhelpful emotions like anger or jealousy. This mental restraint is central to temperance, helping us maintain a balanced, rational perspective even in challenging situations.

Wealth

The Stoics believed strongly in rejecting materialism, viewing it as a distraction from living a virtuous and fulfilling life. They believed pursuing wealth, luxury and possessions could lead to dependency and prevent individuals from focusing on what truly matters – character, wisdom and inner peace. Musonius Rufus, arguably the most austere of the Roman Stoic philosophers, emphasized that although wealth can provide physical pleasures, it can't bring contentment, banish grief or defend us against old age.

Seneca warned against the endless pursuit of riches, emphasizing that true happiness doesn't come from what we own but from how we view and handle life's challenges. Seneca's teachings on moderation and the dangers of wealth were particularly striking – and often controversial – because he himself was extraordinarily wealthy. As an advisor to Emperor Nero, Seneca amassed significant wealth, which raised questions among his contemporaries about the sincerity of his beliefs. However, Seneca argued that wealth isn't inherently harmful; rather, it's one's attachment to it that leads to moral compromise. He encouraged the wealthy to use their resources responsibly, stressing that riches should be managed with discipline and never valued above virtue. For Seneca, wealth was a tool – not an end – and true contentment came from moderation, not indulgence.

Epictetus also believed that material possessions could easily control us if we didn't maintain a disciplined mind, urging his students to see wealth as irrelevant to true happiness. He famously said, "Wealth consists not in having great possessions, but in having few wants."

For the Stoics, practising temperance meant freeing oneself from the grip of material desires, allowing a life focused on virtue and inner tranquillity rather than the fleeting pleasure of possessions.

STOIC FASHION

The Stoics emphasized practicality in dress, valuing comfort over fashion. They favoured simple, functional clothing, such as tunics and sandals, which allowed freedom of movement, reflecting their belief in modesty. Musonius Rufus said, "One should use clothing and footwear in the same way as one uses armour: to defend the body, not to show off." This approach highlights their focus on character rather than superficial appearances.

Avoiding excess

The Stoics believed that recognizing imbalances in our lives – spotting where we have excesses or deficiencies – is essential to cultivating temperance. When we allow any area of life to be ruled by excess, we disrupt inner harmony and lose our freedom. Instead, Stoicism encourages us to find a balanced path: to moderate our desires and impulses to prevent them from dominating us.

Cato the Younger embraced temperance by rejecting the luxuries of Roman aristocracy; he wore simple clothing and often walked barefoot in winter. Seneca, though wealthy, advocated self-restraint, emphasizing the importance of mental detachment from material comforts and a balanced approach to wealth.

Seneca warned that immoderate desires distract us from what truly matters, leading to dependency and dissatisfaction. By examining our habits and recognizing areas of excess, we can restore balance and focus on what genuinely enriches our lives. Epictetus echoed this, advising his students to consider whether they indulged in anything unnecessarily. Temperance, he believed, meant restraining impulses that lead to distraction, allowing for a clearer, more purposeful life.

Humility

Humility is a core concept in Stoic philosophy, and the idea that humility can kill pride is central to it. The Stoics defined humility as recognizing one's limitations, avoiding arrogance and valuing wisdom over status or wealth. This form of self-restraint helped them remain grounded, aware that virtue – not social status, wealth or accolades – was the true measure of a person.

Marcus Aurelius, one of the most powerful emperors in history, exemplified humility through his daily practices. He constantly reminded himself to act with patience and compassion, treating others as equals despite his rank. He often reflected on the fleeting nature of power and fame, focusing instead on his duties as a human being.

Similarly, Epictetus, a former slave who became a respected Stoic teacher, embodied humility and demonstrated through his teachings and actions that wisdom is accessible to everyone, regardless of social standing. He emphasized that external status is irrelevant to one's character, urging his students to practise restraint, avoid pride and focus on inner growth. Through humility, the Stoics believed they could better align with their purpose, maintaining integrity and clarity in every action.

Wake up!

The Stoics believed that early mornings and rituals set the tone for a purposeful day and were essential to developing temperance.

Marcus Aurelius famously wrestled with the challenge of rising early, reminding himself that as humans, our nature is to fulfil our duty and contribute to the world. In *Meditations*, he urged himself to remember how every part of nature fulfils its purpose – the ants, the spiders, the bees, all doing their part, and working for order in the Universe. Humans, too, are meant to work and contribute. For Marcus, the motivation to rise early lay in cooperating with this natural order, giving him the mental space to consider his responsibilities, cultivate gratitude and prepare for whatever challenges lay ahead. Beginning the day with focus and discipline allowed him to resist distractions and thereby practise the virtue of temperance.

Time to rest

The Stoics were early advocates of what we now call "self-care". They emphasized a thoughtful balance between work and rest, considering both essential to a life of purpose and resilience. For them, temperance meant knowing when to engage in focused effort and when to step back for renewal. They understood that constant exertion without breaks could cloud judgement and weaken the mind, while excessive leisure could lead to stagnation and missed opportunities for personal growth. Sleeping and reading were viewed as essential tools for relaxation: restful sleep as a way to restore clarity and reading as a calming practice to nurture the mind and deepen wisdom.

Marcus Aurelius, balancing the demands of his role as emperor with his philosophical reflections, often reminded himself in *Meditations* to pause and restore his inner strength. Similarly, Seneca saw temperance as working in partnership with nature's rhythms of action and renewal. He championed intentional rest as essential for maintaining focus and vitality, writing in *On Tranquillity of Mind*, "The mind must be given relaxation – it will rise improved and sharper after a good break."

Justice

The Stoic virtue of justice is rooted in the idea that we have a duty to act fairly and honourably in our interactions with others. Stoicism teaches that justice is not only about following laws but also about embodying ethical principles that honour each person's inherent worth. For Stoics, justice applies broadly to interpersonal relationships, requiring freedom from anger, envy and jealousy, and embracing all people as equals.

Zeno of Citium was the first philosopher to make duty (*kathēkon*) a central concept. He believed we each have a moral obligation to fulfil our roles within our families and communities with integrity and responsibility. For Zeno, justice was not just a private virtue but also a social one: it required active participation in public life. He taught that, unless physically or mentally unable, each person has a duty to contribute to the welfare of society, promoting a collective sense of harmony and unity.

Seneca expanded on justice by focusing on the inner qualities required for just behaviour. He insisted that a just person must be free from harmful emotions like anger and envy, which cloud judgement and prevent fair treatment. In his *Letters*, Seneca encouraged the practice of compassion and forgiveness, seeing these qualities as essential to treating others with fairness and respect.

Marcus Aurelius also viewed justice as a guiding principle in all human relationships. He believed that humans are social creatures, naturally bound to one another. He wrote, "What brings no benefit to the hive brings no benefit to the bee", illustrating the Stoic belief that individual well-being is tied to the welfare of the community. For Marcus, justice meant treating each person as a valuable part of the larger human family, understanding that true virtue supports not just personal growth but also the common good.

Stoic justice involves more than just observing rules; it requires us to act with genuine care for others and a commitment to uphold equity in every interaction. Through this virtue, Stoicism invites us to see ourselves as interconnected, with a responsibility to treat others fairly and to contribute meaningfully to the world around us.

Stillness

The Stoics valued stillness as a way to cultivate clarity and self-control, linking it closely to the virtue of temperance. By practising this internal discipline, the Stoics believed they could avoid being swept up by emotions and impulses, leading to wiser, more deliberate actions.

The Stoics taught that true stillness isn't found by escaping to the country or changing your life circumstances. Marcus Aurelius frequently reminded himself to find tranquillity within, even amid the clamour of imperial duties. In *Meditations*, he wrote, "There is nowhere that a person can find a more peaceful and trouble-free retreat than in his own mind... So constantly give yourself this retreat, and renew yourself."

Seneca also recognized that people mistakenly believe they need to flee their lives to find peace. In his *Letters*, he advised, "You need a change of soul rather than a change of climate." Seneca practised this by stepping back from his political responsibilities to reflect rather than by seeking to permanently leave them.

The Golden Rule

The Stoic Golden Rule encapsulates the principle of treating others as you wish to be treated, embodying the essence of justice in Stoic philosophy. This ethical guideline emphasizes empathy and fairness, urging individuals to consider the perspectives and feelings of others in their judgements and actions.

Epictetus conveyed this idea when he encouraged his followers to act with kindness and understanding, emphasizing that our shared humanity requires us to treat each other with respect. By adopting this perspective, we can develop a just society where everyone feels valued and understood.

Marcus Aurelius echoed this sentiment in *Meditations*, reminding himself that everyone has their struggles and deserves compassion. He believed that understanding the common challenges faced by others helps to break down barriers and encourages a sense of interconnectedness.

The Stoic Golden Rule serves as an essential guide for practising justice, urging individuals to exemplify the fairness and kindness they wish to receive, ultimately contributing to a more equitable and compassionate world.

Social creatures

Justice, in Stoicism, isn't just about fairness in a legal sense; it's about recognizing the mutual dependency of all human beings and fulfilling our duties to others. The Stoic concept of *oikeiosis* (appropriation) refers to our natural inclination to care for others, which grows as we recognize our shared humanity.

This idea evolved as the philosophy developed:

- Chrysippus introduced the idea of what is "fitting" or "appropriate" (*oikeios*) in human (and ethical) development, emphasizing that it begins with a natural inclination for self-preservation and extends to parental care for children.
- Antipater built on Chrysippus' ideas by linking personal interests to the well-being of fellow human beings, highlighting the interconnectedness of individual and collective good.
- Hierocles, a second-century Greek Stoic, expanded the concept of *oikeiosis* further by extending the personal sphere of care to encompass the social interests of other people. Hierocles pictured our spheres of concern as a series of ever-widening

circles, with our own self (mind and body) in the centre, radiating out to "family", then "fellow citizens", then "countrymen" and finally "all mankind". Hierocles viewed this process as the foundation of moral relationships.

The notion of the *kathēkonta*, those actions which we're duty-bound to undertake, similarly reflects a deep Stoic emphasis on recognizing our part in a larger whole, as described by Hierocles' spheres of concern. This was based on the Stoic idea that human nature is fundamentally rational *and* social. Hierocles wrote, "For this reason, we are eager by nature to win over and make a friend of everyone." We should therefore strive to bring the outer circles (or spheres) closer to ourselves: treat family like you would yourself; treat a friend like family; treat a fellow citizen like a friend; and treat a foreigner as you would a fellow citizen.

> I am a human being; I regard nothing human as foreign to me. Let us hold things in common, as we are born for the common good.
>
> **Latin playwright Terence, in Seneca's *Letters***

Cooperation

Stoic justice goes beyond fairness; it involves working together for the common good. Stoicism teaches that humans are inherently social beings, and living virtuously means fulfilling our role within the broader community through cooperation and contributing positively to society.

As Roman emperor, Marcus Aurelius governed with a deep sense of responsibility to the people. Rather than ruling with absolute power, he prioritized cooperation with his advisors, listening to their perspectives and making decisions that benefited the empire. He often reflected on the importance of working in harmony, reminding himself that all individuals are interconnected and have a role in society's well-being.

Epictetus also emphasized the importance of fulfilling our duties within relationships, seeing them as essential for maintaining the natural order. He taught that every person is part of a larger community, or *cosmopolis*, and that our actions impact others.

In essence, Stoic cooperation was about recognizing that individual virtue is inseparable from contributing to the larger community, ensuring that the common good is upheld.

Sympatheia

The Stoics believed deeply in *sympatheia*, the concept of universal interconnectedness, which holds that all people, and all parts of nature, are interwoven within a greater whole. This sense of unity underpins the Stoic virtue of justice, as it encourages seeing others not as separate or lesser beings but as interdependent parts of the same universe. Justice begins with recognizing this shared connection and treating others with fairness, respect and empathy.

Marcus Aurelius expressed *sympatheia* clearly in *Meditations*, writing that "we were born for cooperation, like feet, like hands, like eyelids, like the rows of the upper and lower teeth". This metaphor highlights the Stoic view that all humans are inherently designed to work together, supporting and benefiting one another. By understanding *sympatheia*, Stoics believed that individuals could move beyond selfish concerns and act in the interest of the collective, fostering harmony.

> The universe that you see, containing the human and the divine, is a unity; we are the limbs of a mighty body.
>
> **Seneca, *Letters***

Injustice

It's easy to assume that Stoicism's emphasis on acceptance might imply indifference to politics or injustice. In reality, the ancient Stoics were far from passive observers. While Stoic thinkers encouraged inner resilience, this was coupled with the idea that we have a natural obligation to stand against harm and promote justice. They believed the virtue of justice called for active resistance to wrongdoing – so long as it was done with rationality and restraint, not anger or revenge.

Roman Stoics, in particular, didn't shy away from condemning the abuse of power they witnessed in their society. Figures like Seneca advised against cruelty and urged rulers towards fairness, demonstrating that Stoicism demands moral courage, even when confronting authority.

> The essence of good is a certain kind of reasoned choice; just as the essence of evil is another kind.
>
> **Epictetus, in *Discourses***

The foolish

Marcus Aurelius was emperor of the world's largest empire at the time, yet he witnessed even his officials speaking and acting thoughtlessly. He reminded himself that even the foolish have their struggles, and we should strive to act with understanding. He wrote, "It's silly to try to escape other people's faults. They are inescapable. Just try to escape your own."

The Stoics, including Marcus, emphasized the importance of maintaining one's composure and integrity even in the face of other peoples' ignorant behaviour. They believed justice involves treating everyone fairly and respectfully, even those whose actions may seem misguided or foolish.

Epictetus advised that rather than reacting with anger or disdain, we should recognize the limitations of others and respond with patience. Seneca said we must not allow the foolishness of others to disturb our peace. He believed that it's our duty to engage with kindness and reason, rather than resorting to hostility.

Generosity

Seneca placed great importance on generosity (*eumenia*) and gratitude. In fact, his longest work that centres on a single subject, *On Benefits*, focuses on these themes. Seneca argued that true generosity arises from a pure intention to benefit others, with the joy of giving rooted in the act itself, not in anticipating something in return.

Seneca emphasized that generosity should not be validated by a third party. He even suggested that a gift, to be truly virtuous, should be given in secret. If we expect repayment, Seneca warned, we are not giving but engaging in a transaction or bribery, depending on the situation.

Seneca stressed the importance of true gratitude when receiving gifts. He viewed ingratitude as one of the worst vices. In this way, Stoicism encourages selflessness and mutual respect, promoting authentic generosity in our interactions.

> Let us give in the same spirit with which we would want to receive – above all, generously, promptly, with no hesitation.
>
> **Seneca, *On Benefits***

Forgiveness

The Stoics saw forgiveness as essential to the virtue of justice, believing that holding onto anger or seeking revenge disrupts both personal peace and harmony with others. Forgiveness, for the Stoics, was about understanding human nature and accepting that people make mistakes – often out of ignorance or misjudgement. They encouraged responding to others' flaws with patience and compassion rather than resentment.

Marcus Aurelius frequently reminded himself to forgive others, seeing it as a way to maintain inner calm and promote justice. "The best way to avenge yourself", he wrote, "is to not be like that [wrongdoer]." He believed that by changing his perception and not taking others' actions personally, he could act more justly and maintain inner peace.

Seneca also championed forgiveness, advocating leniency in judgement and understanding over punishment. In his treatise *On Anger*, he wrote, "Let's be kind to one another. We're just wicked people living among wicked people. Only one thing can give us peace, and that's a pact of mutual leniency." By choosing forgiveness over retaliation, Seneca demonstrated that true strength lies in self-control and empathy rather than in holding grudges.

Role models

The Stoics valued role models as essential to cultivating wisdom. They believed that observing individuals who embody courage, temperance and resilience offers invaluable insights into virtuous living. Seneca, for instance, urged people to select role models who reflect the traits they aspire to develop. He believed that by emulating admirable qualities – without losing individuality – people could strengthen their character and approach wisdom. In his *Letters*, he wrote, "Choose someone whose way of life as well as words, and whose very face as mirroring the character that lies behind it, have won your approval."

However, Stoics cautioned against blind imitation. Role models should guide rather than dictate our every action; their example should serve as inspiration to refine our character and improve our conduct.

Epictetus encouraged his followers to study Socrates' commitment to truth and resilience. Marcus Aurelius praised his adoptive father, Emperor Antoninus Pius, for his patience, temperance and leadership. Seneca's role model was Cato the Younger, who was known for his moral integrity.

STOICISM IN THE MODERN WORLD

Stoicism, a philosophy born in the bustling streets of ancient Athens, has seen an impressive revival in the twenty-first century. Today, it's more than just an idea from history – it's a way of life that's inspiring people to face everyday challenges with greater resilience, clarity and purpose. In recent years, Stoicism has surged in popularity, with countless books and online communities encouraging people to turn to Stoic principles as a path to a more balanced and meaningful life.

In this chapter, you'll explore how this revival in Stoicism began, tracing its journey from ancient teachings to contemporary relevance. You'll discover how Stoic ideas influenced the development of techniques like cognitive behavioural therapy, connecting timeless wisdom to modern methods for managing anxiety and emotions effectively. You'll also look at the impact of present-day Stoics, including Ryan Holiday and Massimo Pigliucci, whose books, lectures and podcasts have introduced a new generation to Stoicism.

By the end of this chapter, you'll understand why Stoicism has re-emerged as a philosophy and practical guide for navigating the complexities of the modern world.

Studying Stoicism

Since the Renaissance (fourteenth to seventeenth century), Stoic insights into the management of harmful emotions – what they called the passions – have intrigued scholars and writers. Justus Lipsius (1547–1606) promoted Stoic resilience to endure life's hardships, while Michel de Montaigne (1533–1592) drew on Stoic ideas to examine the nature of the self, fear and tranquillity.

The philosopher David Hume (1711–1776) examined the interplay between reason and passion, critiquing but also respecting Stoic ideals about self-control, and Immanuel Kant (1724–1804), though critical of Stoicism's emphasis on detachment, valued its insights on moral duty and the power of rationality in moral actions. These thinkers helped shape the intellectual environment that would later influence modern psychology.

Latin education was widespread across Europe during the Middle Ages (fifth to fourteenth century), and the texts of Cicero and Seneca were prized for their style and moral teachings. The two surviving copies of Marcus Aurelius' *Meditations* (written in Greek) were rediscovered in the sixteenth century and translated into Latin in 1558, which helped it reach a broader audience.

Psychotherapy

Stoicism endured for over 2,000 years before its therapeutic principles began to be recognized in early psychotherapy. In the 1890s, Swiss neuropathologist Paul Charles Dubois pioneered rational approaches to psychotherapy, notably through what he called "persuasion therapy". Dubois encouraged patients to challenge their irrational beliefs and justify their negative feelings, drawing directly from both Socratic and Stoic methods. He argued that many emotional and psychosomatic issues stemmed from negative self-talk, or autosuggestions, which could be countered with rational examination. In his 1911 book, *The Education of Self*, he agreed with Seneca's statement that "one exaggerates, imagines, anticipates affliction", and told his patients, "Do not let us build a second story to our sorrow by being sorry for our sorrow."

In 1924, French psychotherapist Charles Baudouin continued Dubois' approach, writing about Stoicism's relevance for modern psychotherapy and self-help. He saw particular value in the Stoic emphasis on self-discipline and "education of the character".

In a 1954 study, German author Paul Rabbow argued that ancient Stoics and Epicureans had effectively prescribed "moral exercises" to their pupils: "procedures or determinate acts, intended to influence oneself, carried out with the express goal of achieving a moral effect". Pierre Hadot developed this idea in the 1990s with his conception of philosophical exercises (see p.116).

The foundation built in the first half of the twentieth century paved the way for psychologists Albert Ellis and Aaron Beck, who developed Rational Emotive Behaviour Therapy (REBT) in the 1950s and Cognitive Behavioural Therapy (CBT) in the 1960s, respectively. Both credited Stoicism as a key influence in shaping their approaches. The Stoic focus on rational thinking and emotional resilience aligned closely with their aim to help people confront irrational beliefs and cultivate balanced, adaptive responses to life's challenges. Beck's CBT incorporated Stoic techniques for examining judgements to identify and reframe negative thought patterns, while Ellis applied Epictetus' assertion that "men are disturbed not by things, but by the views which they take of them", to help clients manage emotional responses through reasoned perspective and resilience.

A. A. Long

In academic circles, particularly in the United States and Europe, courses on Stoicism began reappearing in both philosophy and psychology departments in the mid-twentieth century. This revival allowed Stoic philosophy to be explored as both an ethical system and a framework for mental health, merging ancient wisdom with contemporary psychology. Scholars and therapists alike found that Stoic principles – especially regarding rational thinking, self-discipline and emotional resilience – had profound applications for managing stress, reducing anxiety and fostering mental well-being.

A major factor in this resurgence was the publication in 1971 of *Problems in Stoicism*, a collection of essays edited by A. A. Long. The book looked at the contributions of the Greek Stoics to logic, ethics, metaphysics and epistemology. Long, a distinguished British-American philosopher, presented Stoic ideas with new clarity and depth, connecting Stoicism's ethical insights with modern interests in personal development and resilience. His work not only reinvigorated scholarly interest in Stoicism but also sparked curiosity among general audiences, who found Stoic ideas highly applicable to contemporary life. *Problems in Stoicism* became a key resource for understanding how Stoic principles, such as moral responsibility and excellence of character, could be integrated with modern psychological practices. Long's interpretation made Stoicism more accessible and relevant to a new generation of students and thinkers. He wrote, "During the last few years the tide for Stoicism has happily begun to turn."

Around this time, the rise of virtue ethics as a respected approach in philosophy further propelled Stoicism's revival. Virtue ethics, which emphasizes character development and moral excellence over rigid rules, resonated strongly with Stoic ideas of cultivating virtues. The Stoic model of personal growth through disciplined thought and action appealed greatly to those interested in ethical frameworks focused on character rather than external behaviours alone. This philosophical shift, led by influential thinkers such as Philippa Foot and Alasdair MacIntyre, brought Stoicism back into mainstream ethical discourse.

By the late 1970s, Stoic ideas had not only permeated academic philosophy and therapeutic settings but were also spreading through popular self-help literature. Concepts of emotional resilience, self-control and acceptance, long championed by Stoics, became fundamental in many personal development practices and strategies.

A way of life

In the 1980s and 1990s, Stoicism experienced a resurgence. Scholar Ilsetraut Hadot argued that ancient philosophers served as "spiritual directors", who put shaping character above rhetorical skill – an idea that heavily influenced her husband, the French philosopher Pierre Hadot. His book *Philosophy as a Way of Life* illuminated Stoic practices as effective exercises for daily resilience and self-improvement. He emphasized that Stoicism was less about abstract thought and more about guiding people towards personal transformation. His work revealed how Stoicism can help us "relearn how to see the world" and became globally renowned.

American philosopher Lawrence Becker's *A New Stoicism* proposed that Stoicism could coexist with contemporary science and ethics. His aim was to bring Stoicism up to date and reject the popular view of Stoics as emotionally detached, arguing that modern Stoics can hail from all corners of society.

Since the 1980s, increased gender diversity in academia and broader societal shifts allowed female philosophers to bring fresh perspectives and draw new audiences to Stoicism. Martha Nussbaum, a prominent American philosopher, explored Stoic themes in relation to emotions and ethics. Her work in *The Therapy of Desire* highlighted Stoicism's relevance to understanding and managing human emotions. American philosopher Margaret Graver explored how Stoic principles like the rule of reason can guide us through emotional turmoil, showing how Stoicism's rational frameworks can foster psychological resilience without denying our human nature.

FEMALE PERSPECTIVE

Though female thinkers have explored Stoicism for centuries, their contributions have often gone unrecognized. In the eighteenth century, Elizabeth Carter made Stoic philosophy accessible by translating all of Epictetus' teachings (as recorded by his pupil Arrian) into English. Since the 1980s, increased gender diversity in academia and popular philosophy publications have boosted the influence of women like Martha Nussbaum, British philosopher Julia Annas (renowned for her work in ancient ethical theories) and Margaret Graver, who have brought Stoicism to wider audiences.

Accessibility

For much of its history, Stoicism was taught privately to aristocratic students. Today, widespread literacy and accessible resources have brought Stoic teachings to people from all backgrounds. Since the late twentieth century, Stoicism has experienced a resurgence through translated texts, popular philosophy books and online platforms. Philosophers like Massimo Pigliucci have popularized Stoic practices through online blogs and books, such as *How to Be a Stoic*. Pigliucci's involvement with the Modern Stoicism movement reached a global audience, fostering a global community of practitioners and discussions on living a Stoic life. Now, anyone with access to the internet, a bookshop or a library can explore Stoicism at their own pace.

In a *New York Times* article in 2021, American scholar Nancy Sherman criticized the way in which Stoic doctrines have been reduced to "self-focused pop Stoicism", turning profound teachings into quick "lifehacks" or shortcuts for self-improvement. Ironically, this very trend has increased public awareness of Stoicism, encouraging deeper exploration of its original philosophical depth and meaning.

Stoic Week

Stoic Week started in the UK in 2012 as part of a "Stoicism and Therapy" project at Exeter University. Led by Professors Christopher Gill and John Wilkins, the seminar brought together students, philosophers and cognitive therapists to examine Stoicism's connections to Cognitive Behavioural Therapy (see p.113). The initial interest far exceeded expectations, prompting the launch of Stoic Week to the public in 2013 by the non-profit organization Modern Stoicism. Now a free annual event, Stoic Week invites participants worldwide to engage in daily readings, mindfulness exercises and Stoic journalling. Data from Modern Stoicism reveals that after just one week of practising Stoic techniques, participants report an average 15 per cent reduction in negative emotions and a 14 per cent increase in life satisfaction.

Stoicism has gradually become a unifying force. Initiatives like Stoic Week foster community, while Epictetus' teaching on acceptance echoes in modern support groups, as in Alcoholics Anonymous' "Serenity Prayer" (written by Reinhold Niebuhr in the 1930s): "God, give me the serenity to accept the things I cannot change, the courage to change the things I can, and the wisdom to know the difference."

Ryan Holiday

A distinctive feature of Stoicism's modern resurgence is the role of non-academics in bringing the philosophy to a wider audience. Among them, Ryan Holiday has emerged as a leading voice. At just 19 years old, while working in marketing, Holiday attended a conference where radio and television host Drew Pinsky suggested reading books by the Stoics – a recommendation Holiday later described as life-changing. Books like Marcus Aurelius' *Meditations* and Seneca's *Letters* had a transformative effect on him, inspiring him to shift his career towards sharing Stoic principles with a broad audience.

His 2014 book, *The Obstacle is the Way*, became a bestseller, earning a cult following for its emphasis on turning challenges into opportunities. His books, which include *Ego is the Enemy* and *Stillness is the Key*, have collectively sold millions of copies.

As a former marketing executive, Holiday also understands the power of using multiple media platforms. His *Daily Stoic* podcast and YouTube channel reach vast audiences, providing short, engaging episodes on Stoic wisdom and practical applications. This multi-format delivery has, in turn, helped to shape Stoicism as a toolkit for emotional resilience, leadership and productivity. Public figures have cited Holiday's work as pivotal in their understanding of Stoicism.

Holiday's work marks a significant departure from the philosophy's past, when Stoic teachings were often confined to academic circles or private study. By translating Stoicism into digestible lessons for a modern audience, he has redefined the philosophy as an accessible guide for daily life, showing that Stoic wisdom is not just for scholars.

Critics argue that Holiday's approach repackages Stoicism as a productivity system geared towards high achievers, questioning whether his own success fully aligns with Stoic principles of humility and moderation. Yet, regardless of these debates, his influence remains significant – Holiday has introduced Stoicism to millions who might never have encountered it otherwise. Through his work, Stoicism has moved firmly into the public eye and impacted the lives of countless people from a range of backgrounds.

> I didn't know there was such a roadmap for how to be a good person, for how to be a strong person, for how to be a resilient person.
>
> **Ryan Holiday**

"Broicism"

The influence of twenty-first century advocates for Stoicism like Ryan Holiday, among others, has helped make Stoicism particularly popular among entrepreneurs and tech leaders, especially in Silicon Valley. By the 2020s, the philosophy was increasingly marketed to young men as a guide for resilience and personal grit. This trend – sometimes called "broicism" – highlights Stoicism's teachings on self-discipline, emotional control and mental strength but often oversimplifies its richer ethical foundations. This narrow interpretation risks distorting it into a hyper-masculine "toughness" mindset and brings challenges in preserving the philosophy's deeper nuanced teachings.

Ancient Stoicism emphasizes balance, compassion, nature and the value of interpersonal relationships (see p.101) – principles that extend far beyond productivity. Stoic virtues like justice, wisdom and temperance speak to everyone, not just a single demographic. Today, feminist voices argue that Stoicism offers tools for everyone to live ethically and meaningfully, not merely to maximize productivity or achieve traditional markers of success.

Modern Stoics

Today's world offers us unprecedented power to shape our future. For instance, we know we can influence climate change through collective action. This shift challenges modern Stoics to rethink key principles, such as control and acceptance, to incorporate not only personal resilience but also active responsibility. Similarly, Stoicism traditionally placed high value on rationality over emotion. Contemporary psychology, however, emphasizes that emotions play a critical role in well-being and decision-making. Modern Stoics can incorporate a more balanced view, integrating emotional intelligence with rationality.

With twenty-first-century issues such as ageing populations, artificial intelligence and environmental responsibility looming large across societies, contemporary Stoicism has an opportunity – and perhaps an obligation – to expand its ethical focus. Stoicism's future likely involves a more inclusive, holistic interpretation – one that transcends the recent "productivity" trend and refocuses on its core teachings of ethical living and communal responsibility.

Conclusion

Throughout history, humans have exchanged ideas on how to live well and overcome life's challenges. Among countless debates and doctrines, Stoicism stands out as a philosophy offering practical, timeless solutions. Embraced by emperors and slaves alike, it speaks to all of us, regardless of our circumstances.

This book has introduced you to Stoicism's history, key figures and core teachings, demonstrating how its practical approach resonates across cultures and centuries. However, practising Stoicism is far from easy. At its heart, it encourages self-examination and the cultivation of virtues in our daily lives. In *On the Shortness of Life*, Seneca wisely said, "Of all people only those are at leisure who make time for philosophy, only those are really alive."

Take these insights and make them your own; reflect on your judgements, question assumptions and focus on what you can control. Though time separates you from the ancient Stoics, their philosophy remains a permanent guiding hand towards a life of fulfilment and purpose.

Additional resources

Marcus Aurelius, *Meditations*, translated by Martin Hammond (Penguin Classics, 2006)

Brigid Delaney, *Reasons Not to Worry: How to Be Stoic in Chaotic Times* (Piatkus, 2023)

Epictetus, *Discourses and Selected Writings*, translated by Robert Dobbin (Penguin Classics, 2008)

Ryan Holiday and Stephen Hanselman, *The Daily Stoic: 366 Meditations on Wisdom, Perseverance, and the Art of Living* (Profile Books, 2016)

Massimo Pigliucci, *How to Be a Stoic: Ancient Wisdom for Modern Living* (Basic Books, 2017)

Donald Robertson, *How to Think Like a Roman Emperor: The Stoic Philosophy of Marcus Aurelius* (Griffin, 2020)

Seneca, *Letters from a Stoic*, translated by Robin Campbell (Penguin Classics, 2004)

Nancy Sherman, *Stoic Wisdom: Ancient Lessons for Modern Resilience* (OUP USA, 2021)

Tanner Campbell, *Practical Stoicism* podcast

Ryan Holiday, *The Daily Stoic* podcast and newsletter

Modern Stoicism (modernstoicism.com), free online courses and articles

The Stoic Registry (thestoicregistry.org), the oldest Stoic community on the internet

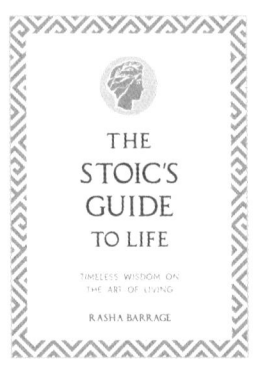

The Stoic's Guide to Life

Rasha Barrage

Hardback • 978-1-83799-360-4

Supercharge your confidence, enhance your well-being and live life as your best self with the help of this modern guide to the ancient art of Stoicism.

Whether you seek greatness or joy, self-knowledge or self-control, the Stoic philosophy can teach you how to exercise the mental muscles you need to rise above everyday stresses and manage whatever life throws at you.

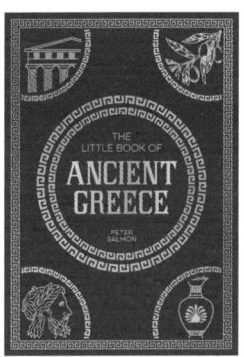

The Little Book of Ancient Greece

Peter Salmon

Paperback • 978-1-83799-535-6

If you've ever been curious about the rich culture and vibrant history of Ancient Greece, dive into this whirlwind tour and discover the highlights of this epic civilization.

Although they lived over 2,000 years ago, the echoes of the Ancient Greeks can still be heard, loud and clear, today. From warfare and politics, to art, culture and everyday life, uncover their history with this fascinating little book.

Have you enjoyed this book? If so, find
us on Facebook at **SUMMERSDALE PUBLISHERS**,
on Twitter/X at **@SUMMERSDALE** and on Instagram
and TikTok at **@SUMMERSDALEBOOKS**
and get in touch.
We'd love to hear from you!

WWW.SUMMERSDALE.COM